RAW MATERIAL:

OPEN THIS BOOK AT RANDOM

TUCKER K. SULLIVAN

Tucker K Sullivan
www.tuckersullivan.com
Instagram: @tuckerksullivan
TikTok: @tuckerksullivan
YouTube: @tuckerksullivan

Printed Worldwide
First Printing 2024
First Edition 2024

ISBN: 978-1-7359585-3-8

Disclaimer: The views, thoughts, and opinions in this book are solely those of Tucker Sullivan. They are weird and possibly incorrect. Reader advised.

RAW MATERIAL:

OPEN THIS BOOK AT RANDOM

Also By Tucker K Sullivan:

Relate! One Human To Another

This Book is Alternately Known As:

100% Biological Human Writing

Fast Food Zen Koans

Non-Sequiturs Only

Literal Rambling

An Accumulation of Words

I'm Not Crazy

A Book for Short Attention Spans

One Massive Poem

Pure Mumbo Jumbo

What is a Non-Sequitur?

"The greatest blessing granted to mankind

come by way of madness,

which is a divine gift."

– **Socrates,** *Divine Madness*

"They called me mad, and I called them mad,

and damn them, they outvoted me."

– Nathaniel Lee

Table of Contents

INTRODUCTION

Hello! The book you are reading almost never saw the light of day. The work in your hands, which I am calling *Raw Material*, was originally intended strictly as a writing exercise, meant only to help me improve my word choice, and test myself as a writer.

I set out with the simple goal to fill an entire spiral bound notebook with lines that I found beautiful or interesting, strictly non-sequiturs, poetic sentences, or word combinations. It was only meant to be writing practice for myself, maybe at best used to come up with some imaginary future book titles, band names, random starting points, scraps of dialogue, or as an exercise to warm myself up before writing a longer 'more substantial' piece.

This notebook was intended to be finished in five years and tossed in the back of my closet, or left in a drawer, never to be seen again. What was meant to be a slow methodical process, to be chipped away at, secretly, in darkness between my other writing projects, suddenly, surprisingly, and completely consumed me.

My past writing style has typically been short poems, between one and ten lines, never anything very long. I've filled very many small pocket notebooks this way, even self-publishing a book of poems (not the best work but I am quite proud of it).

However, I found myself wanting to write even more. The truth is, I felt there was not enough meat on the bones of my previous writing.

With *Raw Material*, I took my old writing style of short thoughts and forced myself to fill the entire page. Rather than writing a few tiny little poems and calling the page 'full', I decided to fill the page, margin to margin, with the same short thoughts.

My heroes are all writers and comedians. Heroic writers, it turns out, tend to write thousands upon thousands of words, ideally millions by the end of their lives. I had yet to really do that. I felt like the notebooks that I had been 'filling up' were lacking. These notebooks had far too much blank space on the page.

While I have not achieved literary greatness, and I'm comfortable in my obscurity, I still have it in my power to do this, to write thousands upon thousands of words (eventually, millions of them). While this is not the longest book ever, it's obviously quite short, while it is not my magnum opus, it is still in my opinion, more *substantial* than the writing that I have done in the past. Also, since I've completed this work, I have sustained a much higher daily word count, which is hopefully leading me to my personal goal of a million words in my lifetime.

There is no story, there isn't even a single paragraph in the meat of book. Instead, it is thousands of words, which I just so happened to find meaningful at the time of writing them. That's it.

Some of the words probably should have been removed, some could have been edited quite a bit better, but all of them had some type of meaning to me at the time that I wrote them. What started as a stupid, throwaway project, turned into a piece of writing that spontaneously *mattered* to me. I hope it matters to some of you brave souls, who have randomly found yourselves reading it.

When I was about ten or twenty pages into this writing practice, I had a change of heart. I realized that I had accidentally written something *kind of cool.* That is my only claim with this book, I will also acknowledge right now that a lot of it is totally stupid, but I did personally at the time, and currently, find the book *kind of cool.*

I tend to forget most of what I write as soon as it leaves the pen, so re-reading this work was like revisiting my own thoughts.

I should also note here, I have worked quite hard over the past five or ten years of my life to make sure that my thoughts are not consistently horrible. This has been a long process of battling suicidal thoughts, neurotic bullshit, and pure delusions, to create a few constructive thought patterns that manage to get me through the day. In the context of maintaining my sanity, writing is my primary savior.

Not all of my writing is written to be read, in fact I think I scrap around ninety-three to ninety-five percent of it. But this book felt like an interesting, maybe even beneficial, thing to share with the world.

I have read quite a few books about writing. Many of them have advised the manic, stylistically sacred practice of *stream of consciousness* journaling, also known as freewriting. This is a writing practice where you let your wrists, your instrument, and your subconscious do all the talking. You just spew out words for as long as you possibly can, with no care for what is coming out and no rules to hold the words back either. You don't worry about grammar, punctuation, form, function, or spelling. This is a writing practice that I admire and cherish. It has gotten me through many cases of annoying writer's block. I often enjoy covering pages in a random and chaotic order. Rather than using the lines provided in a notebook, I've found it helpful to start with the margins, go sideways for a bit, then use the lines until I'm bored with them. While this book was not written in this manner, it was certainly written in that spirit.

Instead, this was a methodical and thoughtful stream of conscious writing practice. I was not rambling, although most of it will definitely read as incoherent rambling. Instead, I was taking my time, making sure that each line had some inherent meaning to me. Rather than let the stream ramble and flow, I practiced with it, forcing it to take some patient steps. I made my stream of consciousness carry its own weight.

There is another reason why I find it worthwhile to publish this work as a complete book, a reason for sharing it with the world. I found that it was a meaningfully mindful practice of writing for myself, so maybe it will inspire some mindfulness in others as well.

I am an amateur practitioner of Zen Buddhist meditation, and I am always looking for ways to help my brain to operate in a less anxious and more mindful way. I found this practice of slowly, methodically, filling this notebook with single thoughts, was enjoyably mindful. It was a different kind of writing than sitting down with a point or a story in mind, telling the story, and calling it a day.

Instead, I would sit and think (or not think), breathe, pray, or meditate, and just write the words that came to mind next. It was never stressful, because in the end the words don't really matter all that much, they don't rely on each other, they don't have to prove some larger point. This lack of rules and simple nature created a mindful practice for myself. I find a similar feeling in the act of re-reading it, so I hope you find the same.

Mindfulness is a true practice, a ritual, a thought process, a verb, a noun, an action, a presence, and a way of being. It is something you can learn about, get better at, and try to incorporate into your life. It is certainly a buzzword of our time, but I think that is because it is truly helpful, and we currently need all the help we can get.

Unfortunately, like many things that are good for us, mindfulness can be difficult to maintain in our world. In our fast paced Western, technology driven world, content is king. We want information instantly, we want to be entertained indefinitely, and God-forbid our phones die. I'm not trying to be overly negative, I use technology as much as anyone, but I'm thankful to have learned some of the principles of mindfulness and incorporated them into my life. I can't call myself a Buddhist or a Taoist, but

I certainly admire these schools of thought, and much of this way of thinking has shaped who I am today.

Writing has always been an act of mindfulness for myself, as well as sometimes the opposite, a distraction from my head. A blank page can be a loud place where I can spew all of my incessant, never-ending thoughts. Despite that chaos, this book has stood out to me as particularly mindful. It was sometimes challenging to sit and write a sentence and immediately let it go. I easily could have filled a page by continuing a thought here or there, but that wasn't the purpose of the exercise. The purpose was to find some beautiful words, write them down, and ask nothing else of them.

So, for the most part, that explains the book. I hope this book will be beneficial for creatives looking to unplug and change their mindset, artists looking for inspiration, writers to chew on the words, and maybe the anxious minded, depressed, or the struggling, to be able to read something positive, that isn't actively trying to kill you.

For any of those who currently find themselves struggling, I hope this book can provide a momentary respite from your troubles. For those who are having a good day already, I hope this book can provide a laugh or an insight, and I hope you continue to have a nice day.

All that the words in this book had to do for me was have just a *little bit* of meaning. I hope you find some meaning in this book as well.

If two of the words rub together to create a spark in your mind, then I will consider the torch to have been lit, and the book to be a massive success.

Writing Constraints

In setting out to fill my notebook with beautiful or thought-provoking words, my goal was *not* to have long coherent thoughts, sentences, or paragraphs.

Instead, I wanted to challenge myself to come up with intricate (or simple) fragments of beautiful or interesting words, with the goal of making myself a more creative writer.

To achieve the desired effect, I decided to limit the punctuation which I would allow myself to use. I separated each fragment of words only by a comma, and I allowed myself only to use apostrophes and hyphens within each segment. No periods, question marks, exclamation marks, semi colons, or any other meaningful punctuation was allowed.

This did leave me with some grammatical errors in the longer fragments, but I decided to keep those errors as they were, in the spirit of the rambling nature of the book.

I did this because I wanted each fragment to stand completely on its own. This made the writing process more of a mindfulness or meditative exercise, rather than a writing project.

If two fragments seem highly related, I tried to separate them in the book. Other than that, I kept very true to the original handwritten first draft of this book. In the process of typing out the original notebook, I made minor changes to the thoughts, but I always kept the style. I also added more rambling as I typed and felt inspired by my own words, which was kind of the whole point.

I also decided to break it up into four chunks which I will designate as these chapters:

☺ *Smiles* ☻

† *Daggers* ⸸

+ *Positive vs Negative* -

♪ *Rhythm* ♫

These chunks are symbolically meaningless, they are only meant to break up the flow of the work slightly.

I wanted to share those rules that I set for myself in completing the manuscript, to provide a better understanding for what you are reading. I consider this a work of poetry, experimental writing, or a mindfulness practice… That's enough talking, here is the rambling…

Now presenting, the most schizophrenic thing I'll ever write.

Smiles

☺

Hospital coffee tastes weird, we left the faucet running and unplugged the refrigerator, an afternoon of picking up wet tattered cardboard off the ground along the side of the highway, planting seeds in sopping fertile mulch, we've agreed to be alone from now on, I'm trying to stop fighting in my head, making my case to my parents like a lawyer, becoming less picky over time, mutual orgasm to death, stethoscope on the side of the road, where did that end up, empty calendar, cool socks, it's not supposed to be good, I like your overalls, there is fresh coffee on the counter, all we have to do is let the paint dry today, I would rather it be painfully loud than deal with this silence, a solitary anomalous experience, we'll be together when it counts, no more pain, a generation of usefulness, pure concentrated flavor, we noticed the clock had stopped ticking, the strange ability to hold one's breath infinitely, the best taco you'll ever have, the absence of quality is highly noticeable, major discovery, we'll pick a starting point at random, we made a connection despite a vast distance, holding concepts in our hands, brilliant simplicity, we felt the airplane stall, we've been given an endless ceiling and the ability to look up, the hammock gently swings, avenue after avenue after avenue, to resonate with many, we are not talking multiple we are talking infinite, we are currently taking those old pictures we're going to look back on right now, yes it is possible, I've finally correctly attuned my ears, your life reads like a novel except every word is true, coming across a massive compendium of useful words, I'm not quite able to say, strive to be smooth not fast, aggressive kindness, what are we supposed to do with all the hatred, switch hands, to perceive what isn't there, tattoo of a treasure map, brute force in a good way, around the body, learning to appreciate your least favorite color, I'll be present in the moment tomorrow, you're bleeding, you were talking in your sleep last night and it made no sense, it should've been easy but it wasn't, it was as sterile as saline in there, we'll just go the other way, feeling well-groomed today, what a greeting, you fogged up the glass, we're in for a circus of pain, fresh veggies from the garden, remind yourself that you're already here, a wonderful sound in a pitch black room, bring your hammer down, yesterday was the present moment too, would you like to go for a walk, we had a little car chase issue, she was more of a backyard cat, I sleep better next to you, that car alarm ruined our quiet moment, literally nothing could have made this any better, I'm undergoing the first electric eye socket installation, we all start out weak and must learn how much strength we have, a deadly crew, catch the quiet cheater, it appears the killer had a well-worn thesaurus, when was the last serious invention, coveted by opposing forces, I saw you looking, we've collectively missed the point, there've been very few of these, keep the spiders they kill the other bugs, expertly trained racoon, covered in bacon and healthy as can be, I'm not scared anymore, perfect placement, have you ever felt like you don't want to fit in to a certain crowd, the admirable act of facing terror, finding a better way to say it, vegetarian conversion candidate, episodic motivation, dream better, remind yourself of what you want to remember, master two opposites, enjoy the planet, I want my shower to feel like a pressure washer, we're dining out tomorrow, no more easy listening, that specific cloud formation speaks to me, turn into the curve, want to go stare at the sun with me, you were never on my side, don't trust anyone saying we could use a good catastrophe, I was awake all day, befriend them, accidental belonging, an obvious clue, alien dog wrangler, finding a unique way to say an old phrase, is there evil behind a good deed the same way there are silver linings to the bad, what is going on with all these sad clowns, emotions that make breathing difficult, space ship security camera installation expert, the American spirit of resisting tyranny, there are places on a chess board that a pawn will never reach but there are promotions too, breaking addiction, living breathing evidence, a constant pressure from within, internal versus external motivation, change your lifestyle to change your life, swimming in an asteroid crater, is there such thing as dangerous information, society typically doesn't look too closely, how much of what we think right now could even be true, a grab bag of assorted concepts, a transition from complete ignorance to total understanding, taking random guesses during a life threatening game, always keep some placebo pills in your medicine cabinet, I love being out of context, they always ruin a perfectly good skyline, if we weren't stuck in our bodies where would you and I float off to, what if we just gave everyone more days off, I'm trying not to do too many questions but they're kind of fun, when you're told you can have as many as you want, as sneaky as carbon monoxide, I would like to sleep as good as my cat just one time in my life, professional nonsense, what am I supposed to believe if my perception is so flawed, take as many moments as you want they are yours, I want to be at peace like a tree, an insane production, the power of flexibility, practicing pirate sailboat maneuvers, do we even have a solid way forward anymore, unleash your unlimited thoughts, searching for the concepts just beyond human understanding but maybe within reach, I would like to live through one or two more paradigm shifts, what are our time coordinates, crash your UAP if you have one, future outcomes are unlimited, saying it isn't possible is annoying, I wonder if I will write the exact same thing twice in this manuscript by accident, every now and again a blessing occurs in our lives, ideas are strange here comes one now, circumstances can be equally good or bad but actions can change circumstances so we should always be focused on our role in the situation in which we find ourselves, I wish I could taste blue the same way I can taste orange, the information creation sector of our economy, don't skimp on your own brain development, we're constantly worried about breaking when our bodies have the miraculous capacity to heal, thinking up a brand new thought experiment, categorical escapism, impossible to define, think all day about growth and healing, do I look like a guy who knows what he is talking about, a demonstrable truth, just drive south for forty three minutes, finish your to do list, realizing crazy is subjective, playing with concepts, every-second-is-a-gift type people, brilliantly ordinary, someone loved everyone, brand new furniture energy, never justify artistry, broccoli is not naturally occurring, swim as deep as you can fathom into cool salt water, every few minutes occurs exactly as it is supposed to, an experiment of emotion, breathe smoothly, if I could make the world ten percent more of anything it would have to be ten percent more kind, battery operated humans, please feed the hungry near you, change your life today, enroll in helicopter lessons, ignore the noise, seek nothing but the truth, when rain dries the ground and a blue sky sends us inside, read voraciously, I broke each of my ten fingers just to feel again, there is factually more to life than this, escape in a golf cart, they don't like my ideas, fairness is key, create your very own gravitational pull, you could always tell, there are worlds that make even less sense than ours, seek and hide, never mind about all the paradigm shifts they are getting hard to adapt to, we don't really have a festival of darkness, it's a matter of fiction, doubling back on your own thoughts, seeking new word combinations, I don't like thinking that everything is a copy of a copy, look no further there has never been a deeper meaning, flexibility is underrated, I wish I paid attention in math class, only prove it to yourself and make your childhood self the proudest, invisible string and burning puppets, bunker builder, there are tunnels under every major institution, it really is a bummer that we have it all wrong, what is the massive void in the Great Pyramid at Giza, taking nonsense seriously, sneaking into a deep underground military base for fun, what lies are we currently propagating, what'll happen when there is no more fertile soil, I think I would rather have an objective reality than have it all be subjective, a comfortable place to sleep, we're witnessing the breakdown of chronological order, weather your own mental storm, the small speck contributed to the massive whole, nothing will ever be quite as spectacular, too complex to repair, we found a burn hole in reality, how hungry are the fish swimming in the sea, I commend your exit strategy, did you feel that magnitude shift, panic is excitement's cousin, they're trying to make stargazing illegal, take your troubles elsewhere, off world operations, reality in context, appreciate your seconds they are useful, there is a chill in my soul, an ever present question, freeze thaw grow, that familiar taste of plastic, the sickness cured itself, the AI is being trained on gigabytes of conflicting data, agitation subsides, a few excellent theories, a mountain looks different depending on which direction you view the peak, I found an address book with just one number in it, the tragedy of the sunken jet ski, pleasant fragrance, apocalyptic recurring nightmares, shatter the boardwalk, jump up and down on a bridge in a flash flood, time discrepancies, put me in a hammock where it's warm, a hundred plus miles per hour alive, shrink your ego, pulled aside and thanked, sharing a couple moments, crash test humans, an allegory about waking up early, an excellent embarrassment, foot massage because feet first, learning to levitate but mangled in the process, you've been heavily influenced by your time zone, I wrote the same exact thing twice pages apart am I going insane, the most minuscule deciding factor, the head of a pin is so tiny how is it even sharp, requirements and conditions, an entire afternoon of thinking, we're onto nothing, we need a bigger bookshelf, a minty fresh take, wonder remains unlimited, life is happening even as we currently talk, I'm trying to achieve permanent flow state, can we just try to reassure each other, taking a few moments to recover, chase after yourself, what happened to all that stuff I was talking about, consider where you're going and walk accordingly, freshly squeezed lime with pure cane sugar, I don't have to listen to you, I'm exercising the language parts of my brain, the memory was the treasure, collapse the wave function, don't forget about your subconscious, a take one leave one economy, we should strive for a post-scarcity world, double or triple or quadruple the meanings, I'll bring you inside my mind so it finally makes sense from the outside, an exponential rise plus a glide, I want to bring those clouds with me, we are the prism, there wasn't a better way this is perfect, cliff jumping this afternoon, knowing beforehand is usually cheating, a paint splattered soul, catch me another time, how you got here doesn't matter it's the moving forward that matters now, as valuable as a full water bottle when you're dehydrated, he finally found the perfect way to say it, place yourself in a comfortable trance, once you're spirit walking you won't remember how you used to drag your feet, the airplane capsized and the sailboat hit a patch of turbulence, training my brain to do anything, be both your harshest critic and your biggest fan, a force of wisdom, it is more fun when there is no clear path, clean sheets and clean socks, adventure cat, demonstrate your magical abilities, do you ever notice you were holding your breath for a little too long, spend as long as you can underwater, some of us came with our purpose but others have to find it, layers of increasingly complex order, no one can assure you of anything, it is imperative that from here on out you make your own way, there is something special about you but someone is telling you there is not, give me a chance and I promise I won't squander it, living proof via daily choices, capitalize your name, face the symphony with no ear plugs, either chime in or listen close, violent inspiration, I'm not happy with my toenail fungus situation, always christen the vessel in good faith, I can tell by the bruising you crash landed here, you can have the skeletons in my closet I don't need them anymore, to achieve desired outcome we must eliminate all other outcomes, I could see my future a thousand miles across the ocean, it was neither a blessing nor a curse, a torn soul stitched back together, you never know which five or six beautiful words you will hear that change your life forever, you'll never think the same way ever again, course correct or die, see I believe in this, the process might fail you, they had to build a massive support beam to hold up the sky, have you ever found a hopeful cynic, chastise the government, break your thumb and slip out of the handcuffs and then climb through an air duct to freedom, you tell me what you see here, horseback riding in low gravity, I can cause a tectonic plate shift but I just don't want to right now, imagine your stuffy nose just went away, we had a bit of a vacuum emergency, the party is just pregaming for the after party, that song came on at just the right time, fresh linen, no one in my circle growing up knew how to play the Pokemon card game but we all just badly wanted all the cards, the official cheddar cheese champion, dump all your skill points in defense and honor, I'm chasing that feeling of I never really thought of it that way, practice proves proficiency, I want to coach a championship team and give a halftime speech or a speech after a tough loss, don't be where you don't want to be, do what you want especially if doing what you want somehow helps others, unfortunately I never really found an underlying theme, I know you can't possibly take any more but here is more, you might see everything clearly for a second or two, brain panic, you'd be surprised how many people have never plumbed their depths, I just want to tell you that you can, one man's recyclables are another man's Tupperware, course correction ability, I can't stop slipping into fractal tangents of thought, we all went beyond the rabbit hole once and now we're here, I think we all agreed to the ground rules before starting life, think about the sheer amount of it all, fragments of varying sizes all hinting towards the existence of a whole, you can have my dreams for me, we can argue over our existence or we can find evidence that explains just a little bit more of it, we'll never know if we can perceive it all but we're guaranteed a little piece, your brain is safe now, mindfulness adds extra flavor, excuse me why do you have this body bag, imagine if these opposing forces reconciled, face forward and then add motion, technically the Earth could crack like an egg, you don't know what I know but I don't know what you know so we could either tell each other that we know nothing or we can converse and discover what the other knows, if I had a bag of diamonds I would scatter them in the strangest places I could think of, beautiful word combos, I don't remember the story but I'll remember the lesson forever, we've got absolutely everything to prove, a concerted conscious clear effort, what you consider a gamble is actually a sure thing, thought provocateur, time travel to the past and invest in your future, I'm hoping I have a word or two worth saying, we need to invest in a better future, I was never one for the three pointer, be present, it really seems like there's never been a beginning or an ending, I'm hoping I have a word or two worth saying, can you say you've mastered a craft, do not ignore the implications of the effectiveness of sunlight, did you catch that fragrance that just wafted by, a swimming pool at the perfect temperature, half a turkey club in the fridge, secure the funds, you wouldn't believe the power of the afterglow, if I'm not part of a larger process then I'll just make my own process, search out life experiences which you can say you're better off having experienced, at least that silver lining was obvious, I would like to live in a place with a cross pollination of different belief systems, spend some time around palm trees when you can, you're purely and uniquely human, search out the interesting real world use for poetic devices, we should allow dolphins and elephants to have a say in what goes on here, sadness can be hard to overcome, I'm at the point where I want to surrender but my hands hurt so bad from holding on that I'm having trouble opening them, a complete remodel of your soul, relying on luck where skill was lacking, place a bucket under the leak in your stream of consciousness, learn how to consistently change your headspace, you are my favorite out of all of them, the chicken cocked its tiny head and wondered if I was looking at it for dinner, we can all fly but we forgot how, thank God for all those reinforcements in all those important battles, go finish a twenty year project, quit vaping, start leaving detailed notes of how you feel right now for your future self to find, careful with those aggravated imaginings, frequenter of dreamscapes, a reasonably priced vacation, are there any empty views, you can consider that done, she could smell the falsehoods and taste the truths, saline for the subconscious, can you feel your reason for being here approaching, a few of these are definitely just for me, we need to treat ourselves better, if the possibilities are endless then what are we going to do with this forever amount of time we've got, by the time you get through all the latitudes you're going to have to tackle the longitudes, you can't show depth without going down, look me in the eyes and tell me our time wasn't any good together, you can just have all of me, how many things in this world would you snip off your pinky finger or a toe for, can someone please invent an effective cure for the sore throat, we are leaving fingerprints spread everywhere across this life that we are living, a place where everyone knows your name and no one has a bad thing to say, light is busier with its frequencies than we will ever perceive, it was simply undeniable, keep multiple irons in the fire and a consistent powerful strike of your hammer, did you lose your childlike wonder and how much time do you plan to spend getting it back if you did, seriously please try to catch me on the other side, a fresh full cup of coffee, when you're lost in thought but regain your bearings and make it out alive, I'm counting on creating a few finished products, study the paint splatter for signs of life, technicalities matter, a run down house with a brand new kitchen, make enough room in your life for the improbable to happen, strength under pressure, a chemical burn right between the eyes, it would be a tragedy to go through life without a single mystical experience, casually planning for complete and utter chaos, it is harder than ever to walk where no one has gone before but each of us still has the powerful desire to go there, never worry about perfection, when the depression moves from my bones into my veins I start to worry, sometimes I wish I had a better way to explain myself other than all these metaphors, the fish is eternally grateful you were a catch and release fisherman, just punch clean through the drywall that'll show 'em, finding out you were unhappy in retrospect is part of the maturation process, I will never feel the condensation from the gasses of Jupiter on my human skin, we stumbled on a well provisioned bunker during post-apocalyptic scavenging, life gets more and more real the further into it you go, an organic set of occurrences, I can't read my own handwriting, a baseline of quality to either uphold or raise, a seeker of spectacles, be spontaneous today, if I can't tell you I'll have to show you, I barely exist as it is, there was a time when you made all the difference, I can't escape this permanent argument going on in my head so I'm forced to just write down some of the better points each side makes, a clean and deliberate process, you can either fear or embrace the inevitable, I've discovered a perfect hide and go seek location but I can't tell anyone where it is, little to none but maybe some, I could feel the wrong words coming out of my mouth but I was forced to listen to them in horror along with everyone else as I spoke them, I personally guarantee you there will be blue sky tomorrow, can you tell he's been at it again, can you feel your new mindset changing you, watch your life for discrepancies, I'm hoping to be noticed, I finished a good book today, broken clavicle, the cut on my hand finally healed, find a healthy obsession, we woke up early and drove to Maine, I had my doubts but she rose to the occasion, you're not me, for some reason finding a person who experienced a similar pain to your own makes it hurt a little less brutally, to receive a passing grade when you thought you'd failed, go do what you've been saying you want to do, wouldn't it be cool, the sheer numbers, assault with a deadly spoon, just because you started out one way doesn't mean you can't go any other ways, genuinely different, appreciating each tiny piece, if the astral plane is real would you like to meet up there next Saturday, collapsing pockets of the multiverse into one another endangers the whole, nothing is less punk rock than saying something that is punk rock isn't punk rock, if you are currently suffering from limited external options it might be time to explore your unlimited internal options, if you're faced with the difficult realization that your dream is completely impossible it might actually be best to just ignore that feeling, the ultimate buzz kill, that couldn't have gone any smoother, the value of a crumb, when you can really milk your own time, what looks like failure to some looks like the first lesson to the successful, if there is emotional intelligence then you should be able to increase your emotional vocabulary, you place your own values and discern your own meanings, line drive base hit to right center field, my three sixty degree high definition video camera got salt water in it and fried the battery, we could see that ending coming, trying and miserably failing to get your point across, do whatever you find that makes your time fly, we think that flowing like water is easy but take a look at the intensity of that current, the other forms that I end up taking will probably find this one funny, we're faced with an overwhelming number of directions but only one of them is ours, the significance of the crash, have you ever been in a bad mood and bumped into someone who is just happy to be here, quietly and politely listening to Notorious Thugs in public sipping a rum spiked dirty chai latte, I can feel you thinking you're better than me, a loud gang vocal chorus, our outcomes are undetermined, failing to account for infinity, eliminate your closed off attitudes one by one, almost all I do is speak figuratively, what is your favorite segment of your life so far, as soon as you tell me I'm not allowed to is when I want to, immune to the effects of empty space, a daring thought process, purify your intentions with powerful ultraviolet light, contribute whatever little you might be able to, learning to allow the flow to pour forth, decentralized yet coordinated, what will come after facing your fears, listen close to when you find yourself in agreement to large concepts, all my heroes write multipage long but perfectly grammatical sentences, your building years will become your foundation, today we solidify our place in history, when taking a leap of faith you tend to worry whether or not you'll survive but once you dive you will either find the water warm and blue or freezing cold and deep green, having just enough time to be able to take your time, I'm not sure when the time will come but I'm committed to going when it finally does, what are you currently making inevitable for your future, there is a small part of me that wants to destroy a dam and watch the damage down river, please prepare me for the large groups of people you bring me into, the majority of knowledge lies in asking the right questions, every speck of paint was a piece of the eventual full body of work, learning to think in a certain style, overlap between seemingly disparate and very far apart ancient cultures, the numbers always speak for themselves if you can read them, you have to give yourself the opportunity to rise to the occasion, if the words are ancient but they still ring true we should really listen close, we are just a small part of the teeming of life taking place on this planet, I was crushed, a mango smoothie on a ninety degree day, due to daily unseen heroic actions we are able to enjoy a slight and temporary peace of mind, and that was the day that I began hiding my feelings about the world, you were one of the only ones who ever understood, you can lead a charge with any mob you want if you know how to whip them up, if it is all temporary then let's cherish the good and let the rest slip away, the impact of some electric keys and a metronome beat, do you talk about the future and your potential with your friends, I hate when all I hear from someone are complaints, a cruise ship on cruise control with no passengers, all I want to do is write books, the infinity of space multiplied by the eternity of time to the highest power of however many dimensions there might possibly be, a masterful mosaic of blues and greens, progression through the wavelengths, I wonder how much buried treasure is still buried out there, I wonder at what specific point in my life becoming an astronaut was eliminated as an option for me, imagine accidentally inventing a history-changing-paradigm-shifting-brand-new tool, I dreamt that I scored a Super Bowl winning touchdown last night, we love the underdog because that is exactly what we are, never judge another's pockets with your feet up relaxing, I can't assure you of much but I can assure you that it'll all only be what you put in, I have a steel splinter between my toes and blood pouring out of my broken nose but the pain of defeat makes any injury that I could possibly suffer feel like minor discomfort, you tell me what is worth erasing, an old rotary phone was the only connection in or out to the world going on outside, the importance of starting with nothing, cactus growing where they shouldn't, chugging along at a proper pace, deep sea diving just to be alone, I could float in this pool all day, it is impossible to know if you have what it takes until you hold what it takes in your hands, stop staring at me, the more you pile on the stronger I become, that toenail fungus is finally gone, an anvil over the head is a perfect metaphor, what will you conjure up into our shared reality, make yourself dizzy and then try to swim the English Channel, the longer you are not bothered the stronger and stronger you become, at the service of the alpha and the omega, what's your life melody, who are you supporting if you are only as good as your support structure, she felt badass just walking around, what I wouldn't give to spin through the air doing multiple flips, win the face off, look how the frozen flow creates the icicles, our sole purpose is to process and build, a pure intention unlocks limitless possibilities, you're not challenging yourself enough, eventually even the most complicated lessons make perfect sense, strengthen the muscles around your weakest point, staying out of conflict is a wise action, jumping into ice cold water is an important rush for you to seek and understand, if this isn't all some elaborate test or experiment I really have no idea what it could be, swimming with iguanas, forget about the wheel look at the genius of whoever invented the shoe, your massive life change might occur both gradually and drastically, worst case scenario you have a negative influence over your shoulder constantly telling you that your goals are stupid and unattainable, I really don't give a shit what is most likely or least likely, never let them rob you of your outlook and replace it with theirs, light to dark and back again, you're a force of nature through your frontal lobe alone, for me success in life would be creating a message that reaches through the negative cloud and positively changes an individual mindset, it's all pretty obvious, at last I'm sleeping sound, a fresh take on old news, find the source of your gravitational pull, can you at least see seeing through a new perspective, never be rude to the staff, eventually you have to learn to stick up for yourself, no one repairs things anymore, I was school in school high, it looks like I'm going to get through my whole life having never committed arson, we should change the borders of every country just for fun, you need to be able to do it just for the sake of doing it, please leave your ulterior motives at the door, if you're running out of things to do I'm sorry to tell you but you're just not being creative enough, understanding the worst is the most effective way to learn about the best, letting the adjective be the noun, always keep one in the chamber, don't let the story conclude until you've understood the message, what is the most superior ice cream flavor, the conspiracy of the change in the color of the sun, I'm sorry I was someplace else, climb up the mast and dive into the sea, the more miracles we ignore the fewer will appear, when the planes cease to fly and the swimming pools are dry, one day this will all be buried, this dumbass tried to steal a hot air balloon, one of my cats plays fetch and the other watches TV, as effective as a sober bartender, don't walk into a restaurant five minutes before they close, of all the things to get good at it seems I've picked incoherent rambling, in order to succeed in this life you must be willing to steal the crown jewels from Buckingham Palace or some crazy shit like that, I could use a cigarette but I'm trying not to, if you're a poet be careful trying to be like Bukowski, a catastrophe at a wedding, close your eyes and have an orgasm, fictionally kill a top general and get away with it, borderline sketchy material, living by the edge of a knife, shooting guns in the air to celebrate, honor your craft and water the grass, you might never know what I'm thinking but I'll work very hard to get you close, from my vantage point I see no other way, I would love to be a cat for a little while, television programming made specifically for psychopaths, I never knew what was meant by the term grandstanding but it sounds rude, I'm happy with whatever future I get because I've come to really appreciate my present, is there anything more we can do, I don't want to do what I'm supposed to do but what I'm SUPPOSED to do, half-assed-half-finished projects, writing is easy but finishing writing anything is damn near impossible, your jeans are in the dryer, what is the point of any kind of thinking other than wishful thinking, this game still has some balancing issues, she only hangs around for so long, the only way to see your future is to bring it to your present, I still can't figure out why I believe in myself, bare feet or sandals for two weeks straight, imagine a version of every single animal domesticated as well as our beloved dogs and cats, the words just started spilling out of my mouth, fortunately and unfortunately are very hard to tell apart from here, I think too much punctuation would take away from some of the meaning in these words, sideways couldn't have a better outcome, there is a correct way to breathe, I'll be working on my faults as best I can, back to the barter system we go, I don't know why I haven't tried that yet, I will work on that, if you don't like it here you can always try someplace else, it is shocking how much gets thrown away and the fact that we can just hop in most dumpsters if we want to, don't judge self-publishing, please invite me to your doomsday bunker house warming party when the time comes, imagine taking the reins for Santa Claus, maybe someday we'll stumble on a better way, thankfully there aren't any enormous carnivorous species of birds, a demonstration of your inner world, if our memories were shorter we would look at each night differently, more power to whoever but I'll gladly stay out of that one, we're not entirely aquatic but we're capable of exploring the surface, I have more to give than this, my entire goal is to broaden and deepen my thoughts, speak of the edge of a cliff into a massive void, you never have to finish the conversation with yourself, there will come a point where there is no fighting left, I've found my place, in essence it was beautiful, don't be afraid to push a broom, careful leaving what you wish you said unsaid, I'm glad that there is always more to every story, why did the number two pencil become so ubiquitous, I hope I get at least a B- on this book, you'll never really know when you're approaching your end but we might never really be finished, if I could show my old self what I'm working on now, an old shed full of toys and sports equipment, feels like light years ago now, it felt a bit lighter before, with care we can grow as the seasons change, you got your point across, the perfect smelling candle, I'm chasing that feeling when you can say I haven't looked at it that way, I haven't showered in four days, he thought he had something with this garbage, I have a critical head in my voice telling me I'm worthless but I've learned that its not very constructive, what am I supposed to do with the feeling that I'm doing everything completely wrong, I would like to dream another dimension but I have trouble sleeping, if I can't be honest in a book I'm writing I guess I'll never be honest anywhere, one of my biggest issues is hearing conflicting advice, I can feel myself being an idiot in the moment, all you'll have left is your awkward self so you better learn to love it, I just noticed that the pit in my stomach went away, we found a crumb of gold in the carpet, the best proof is self-evident, they were not judging you when you thought they were, if today had a favorable outcome what'll we do with tomorrow, we need the word if but I kind of want to eliminate it from my vocabulary, without googling what do AM and PM stand for, I would love to see a linguistic analysis of nonsense, searching for a sober psychedelic mind fuck, strategic impurities, okay I'll stick up for myself now geez, we don't build megalithic structures like we used to, if we were all on the same page none of us would be here, the perfected science of a grilled cheese and tomato soup, looking for meaning and coming up with zilch, we're living under some of the most important and influential lies that have ever been told, rub the dust between your fingertips, as long as I never get a beer belly ah wait never mind, go further into the space where it all feels unreal, how am I supposed to take my time when a law of nature is that we're running out of it, an orchestral cell phone ring tone, I feel like I heard quantum immortality mentioned in a movie or something, by the time I prove my point hopefully I'll be on another point, I don't really want a drastic change but I'm starting to need one just to sustain, stuck in a negative revenue cycle, born with debt, not listening is honestly better than only listening to deflect or manipulate, a concentration of valuable points, the taste of envelope glue, my kitten made my day better, if I'm going to pour my heart and soul into anything it might as well be this, a shower sometime between midnight and two AM, we can all admit that was atrocious, I have no interest in getting away with murder but I wonder if I could, that part was alarming, there is a big swell coming in next week, I could have flipped the car with all of us in it, now is not a good time to rupture my spleen, we may never fully understand what goes on in the feline brain, telling them I was doing it on purpose when I wasn't, escape into a game of pond hockey, lets argue until the sun comes up, give me a cigarette, patterns will emerge, all that and a bag of Cape Cod dark russet potato chips, land a kickflip before you die, feeling good even after the novelty has worn off, these microwave burritos might be the death of me, both practice and commitment are required for achievement, extra sugary cotton candy bubble gum, the flavor profile of life increases as you increase your appetite, our cats like our new carpet, I can read the message intended behind the paint splatter but I'm not sure if I can translate it, it is hard being stuck in the back of the car and never getting your point across, think of how elaborate the stories of reality actually are, I would like to help a few people realize they are worth the energy currently needed to hold their atoms together, if you can find no purpose then you're free to make your own, falling deeper into a fantasy, its funny how reality makes us wonder about what isn't real, you'll have to do all the learning yourself but the universe will provide the lesson material, its funny that the message is clear as day but only if you're looking, I think some paradoxes are necessary for the rest of existence to make sense, I currently can't explain it any better than this, I wonder if I'll ever see the Mona Lisa, many of these life pressures will not go away, I think my blood sugar is dropping, what should you collect for the next forty years, the last two years have taught me to believe in myself and its really not as bad as my anxious thoughts would have me believe, a dog is barking in the next room, trust me, can we just bring gifts to all our enemies and say we're sorry, just want to do better, try folding laundry with an energetic kitten, a nerf gun permanently at the ready, I'm certain there is somewhere I belong, there is an extraterrestrial over my shoulder approving my every decision, hard work with very very little to show for it, can you believe such a thing, I feel like sometime in the past ten years it became less socially acceptable to talk about the elite secret societies ruling the world and deep underground military bases, my favorite fiction rides the line between what is and isn't true, brain computer interfaces are no different than installing a radio antenna into your head just to listen to AM talk radio, going from a suspicion to fully convinced there is more to life than all this, satisfactory progression of events, I can't tell if there is room for me so I'll have to carve it out, part of this is just developing a strange way of talking, you can share your snide remarks with me I find them funny, who invented perforated edges, I wanted to be an inventor when I was a kid, how to think bigger, spending all day thinking of good endings for made up stories, what will accidentally happen next, animals understand more of the big picture than we do, it's funny to think a flamingo evolved naturally, I used to think wall to wall carpet was cool but now these home improvement shows act like it's a bad thing, I trimmed my bush for the first time in months, letting your mind wander means you have full confidence it won't get into anything it shouldn't, coming up with one or two words that say a lot, want to hang out and talk about what we think might happen over the next ten years without getting sad or angry, exploding basketball, genre bending, PhD in gobbledygook, it is interesting that there appear to be universal laws governing us all, I'll be the first to admit many of my beliefs unfortunately conflict, my favorite junkies are probably adrenaline junkies, blatant lack of self-care inevitably leads to some form of self-harm, some mindsets might be easier to change than others, its hard growing up and finding out everyone is hurting, I really hate when there is only so much you can do, passing a drug test and staying clean for good, today I'm going to sit with all the emotions I've been running from, to tell you the truth I'm afraid, it's a trapeze act just to get through the day these days, relinquish all control and see where it goes, powder day, its useful to say in other news in an awkward situation, I kind of feel like darkness is an illusion, do the news casters ever get upset about what the overlords are making them cover, the best I could do was bad, there is a skill you don't know you have yet and you won't know until you try, there is so much more we could have been taught in school, there is no guarantee an alien intelligence has to come from outer space, reminder to use a coaster on the coffee table I always forget, I could use a massage, I feel like bits and pieces are missing, when the truth goes against the available evidence, what you're describing is horrendous, dog farts are always funny, what I wouldn't give to float in space, how did they get everyone to stop smoking cigarettes inside, can I wear my pajamas to work today, all that can be said with just a little eye contact, fresh morning coffee, I'm going to ruin your original hardwood floors, are we excited about our future yet, merino wool base layers, I was going through my normal week when I was hit with an overwhelming sense that I should be doing more, brain back on cruise control, I want to send an old snowmobile off a cliff, only worry about incremental changes, course correct your life, looking for a coupon for fifty percent off helicopter lessons if anyone has one, our society does not prioritize laying in a hammock for hours the way it should, you can always hit reality in the corner with a hammer to shatter the glass and escape, this is the year we face down every one of our fears, it changed my life when I realized you can just trust your brain to do its thing, don't lie, when you make it you will really understand why it was so important that you didn't quit, delay your gratification so far that you barely care about outcomes at all, if you ever run out of topics to talk about with me that is a very bad sign, I felt like I was behind myself watching a movie of everything I was doing and it was all on mute, following that I just wanted to die, typically I can find an interesting aspect of anything but man is this boring, look up shrimp farming and become a millionaire, if your depression is coming from the feeling that you should be better that might actually be a secret weapon because some people are completely fine with being stagnant, I started showing up for myself and suddenly life took off on its own, casually mentioning the nuclear launch codes in conversation, some if not many million dollar ideas were either overlooked or openly called stupid at first, a real good chicken marsala can turn the tide of your whole month, I am currently planning to steal a UFO from the government, we had a full consecutive month of close calls, the funny thing about opportunity is you're not going to predict it, allow yourself the room to work, I may be out in the middle of the ocean but I finally have a chance to ride a current, with just a slight refocus all became clear, stumbling on Manhattan project level secrets, I miss those daydreams I used to have in my desk at school, my current challenge is attempting to put the constant flood of words in my head onto this page somehow, sharing the WiFi password without typing is a great invention, either let yourself down or jump out and see if those wings are any good, don't forget daily practice of your craft, ice cold corona on a beach somewhere, I've grown to appreciate that feeling of wondering whether or not I'm going to make it because that feeling indicates to me that I'm actually trying for once, a tear rolled down my cheek as I lied and said I would call back tomorrow, it is a wild feeling going from wanting to die to wanting to live, it can all fall apart quicker than it takes to build it up so get used to building, pay attention to where the sunlight is hitting your life, more than a few of these are specifically for you, learn to feel that ecstatic feeling, familiarize yourself with paragliding and kitesurfing equipment, struggle is a constant theme in the story of growth, I will never be able to tell you quite what this is, maybe I'll start drinking smoothies for breakfast in my thirties, artists are no longer competing with each other but the instant output of advanced supercomputer artificial intelligence and a society hungry for mindless content, my goal for this project is a combination of nonsense and sense, clarity can come from a good point or a good optometrist, we are the Wikipedia generation, asking more questions than ever, what do you personally plan on doing with the vast amount of knowledge at our fingertips, where do you find yourself placing your most heartfelt and genuine appreciation, there is taco stuff on the stove if you're hungry, cultivate a positive energy to your presence, the expertise demonstrated by switching from fast to slow and back again, pre-order my nothing here, someday someone will take the perfect shot, live each second as a testament to the life you want to live, look at the last five years and then the next five years and then panic, I cleaned the whole house today, we always think about our own personal gravitational pull but what about our tectonic plates and ionosphere, unfortunately I have medically thin skin,

I have a big problem with city planners that seem to completely disregard traffic patterns, aggressive vegetable eaters, rUnNiNg iNtO a PrObLeM iS jUst RuNnInG iNtO a SoLuTiOn shut the fuck up, I cannot guarantee anything in this book is any good, she laid out the deepest eye roll you've ever seen, it's not that I woke up on the wrong side of the bed it's that I was rolled up in the sheets and stuck for the whole day, I'm actually figuring it out now rather than just saying I'll figure it out eventually, my favorite sequence of events to ever occur, if anything just double down on yourself, take a dream walk with me on the next full moon, literary shamanism, the unending quest to develop a semblance of what might one day be called talent, saying your prayers angrily under your breath, I've yet to bleed for it but I fully expect to, it feels important for me to do what I want to do at this point in my life, you might have to go against your old words in an attempt to live more truthful life, I highly recommend filling water balloons with your favorite color paint, you'll think much clearer after you've lost your mind, the balance of growing through critique while ignoring unnecessary nay sayers, strive for resolution, revive your lost dream, we just started passing around a handle of Tito's, you really will never experience your best if you've never experienced your worst, last year was hard on everybody, artificial intelligence couldn't give me what my brain could, the weirdos congregate en masse and the normal people are starting to worry, she lays down in the most uncomfortable looking spots she can find, illegally climb radio towers, I promise it is heavy satire, freedom of thought will eventually develop opposing schools of thought, it hurts when your intuition is wrong, my goal is to dig deeper and reach higher than what I think currently possible for myself, I can't guarantee that I'll keep my future but I know at least right now I have one, countless inadvertent positives, I would like to increase my possible thought complexes through new facts and consistent imaginings, a cock eyed public defender might be a bad sign, I don't want to offend anyone but also getting offended is really no big deal, reasonable people went extinct, whoever said practice makes perfect was lying, I would like to go someplace uninhabited by man, appreciate every micro second, keep your promises, prove to yourself your own ability to deliver, blow your mind daily, learn your capabilities and then increase them, any one of us could be going about our day normally only to be struck down by an apocalyptic vision that we then are tasked to warn the entire world about, I never slept so good as that one fever dream I had, when humanities worries about the end of the world reach a boiling point we just start tearing it all down, they take down all the YouTube videos about the secret tunnels, it is remarkable how much there is in the world that we have absolutely no explanation for, I hope the artificial intelligence engineers aren't using too much Russian dash cam footage as training material, the mystery and miracle of this condition we call life has been keeping me up at night but in a good way, some of you have never smoked salvia out of an apple before a school field trip and it really shows, if only I could still be lulled to sleep, any kind of crash course seems pretty fun, why did you have to say it like that, too short to even be a non sequitur, be the first one to believe in what you're doing and quickly you will find a second and a third, set your own milestones, wouldn't you love to know how all of this came about, learn to sit with your most uncomfortable feelings, the philosophy that underpins it all, enlarge the framework you are using to think, searching for a more appropriate way to say mindfuck, there is an idea that I haven't had yet that hopefully will blow my own mind, my prefrontal cortex is on holiday, if I found what works for me I hope you can find what works for you, when is the last time you were really on a roll, I remember the smell of an entire street from this one bakery in New Bedford, writing the way Pollock painted, I don't trust the traditional route anymore, what are all the VCR repair men doing now, I can't believe some people sell their secrets, a perfectly manicured front lawn, the mistakes made by practiced hands occur for different reasons than the mistakes of a pure beginner, I want a house with red brick floors, boredom has the potential to bring you wherever your interest sparks, what will remain when we boil down our essence into a sticky sauce, it can be nearly impossible to admit you are having trouble, caring for an animal can save your life, remember we can discover things about ourselves so who's to say how close you are to your next discovery, this is the kind of stuff that should probably just stay in drawer for a few years, is there a part of yourself that you could confidently call dynamic, find what is worth your heart and soul because this world will take them eventually, I need a new wallet, every now and then we come across a helpful soul, for every person tearing you down there is hopefully another who would kick their ass, clean socks and underwear, easy does it, jumping up and down on the thinnest ice we can find, understand the most basic components, you could do this way better, embrace the toil when the toil is worth toiling for, you might have to be aimless for a while before you pick the correct direction, find a better way to say it, finding out what is truly best for you is a lifelong process, if that is help then I don't want help, it is not easy to crawl out of a hole, overshoot your dreams, what goes on beyond our wildest fantasies, I can feel how little I know in my daily process of thinking, we are quickly running out of places on this Earth where we can drink the water right from the source, I'm giving myself something to be proud of, I only have the smallest idea of the unspeakable pain that exists in this world, fine tune your inner monologue, it really wouldn't surprise me to find out absolutely no one is in charge and we're on a wild rollercoaster ride and calling it history, there are a huge number of people doing their best to leave a positive impact on this damaged beautiful world, the safety of thick skin, don't puzzle away the meaning, the drama and tragedy played out by reality pierced by occasional comedy, have you ever watched a cliché appear right before your eyes, communication has always been key, forget me tomorrow, there are always further and further developments, the last blessing was not in disguise instead it came with a bullhorn announcing its arrival, quadruple steeped chamomile tea, hiding my plan for world domination in plain sight, are you ready, I really don't know what to do, there will come a time and that time will come to pass too, what can I do in the grand scheme of things that might positively help the grand scheme of things, we have chaos and order for all the same reasons, check your mental inventory, I believe the process you are looking for is known as transcendence, learning that you freeze under pressure is just a valuable lesson for the next crisis, for some reason the last five percent of the journey always feels like forever, just because you wrote all of that doesn't make any of it good, I brought you a breakfast sandwich, the timeline is wishy washy, I want more than scraping by, you'll go from wanting someone to believe in you to the terror of possibly letting them down, crispy potato pancakes, if I'm ever lost in thought I hope I'm smart enough to draw a map, regenerate your ability to feel feelings, I have a feeling I'm going to catch a lucky break this year, it might be safe to say it has all been building up to this very moment, he always kept his word, I just want to feel like I'm doing what I was put on this Earth to do, cats don't grow on trees, think of how much you'll actually get done when you fully embrace the process, I'm more interested in why we are here than arguing over what is right and wrong, I think I'm better off being included with the craziest of the crazy, try to be your best self even in your worst situations, I know I am asking you to do something difficult but it's only because I believe you can rise to the occasion, you'll be surprised how many people doubt you when you start the path towards your dream but that's okay, I won't know if my advice is any good until I've followed it myself for a few more years, I want to build my own superhighway where I want to go, you might be holding your emotions underwater and that's why you're short of breath, why do we want instant gratification when delaying it provides fulfillment, a lot of our world makes no sense, I had a productive day today, we film our lives now because our memories are so flawed, here we are and there we go, the worst part is the constant inescapable feeling that I'm not doing enough, I believe in myself now and I can really tell because I didn't before, lay out in the sun like a reptile, we stumbled upon the perfect parking spot, tell me, if chat GPT could write it then I don't want to, there is no rubric or syllabus to this life, if I could make you understand I would but sometimes I feel like I can't, the daring rescue of a lost cause, I admire the aspirations, if the wind blew stronger we would be building stronger houses, twelve different meanings that I can count, help me understand when I don't, pleasing to the heart and mind, intentional gibberish, stick your feet in ice cold water, fleeting and unexpected joy, when the Keurig coffee maker first came out I thought you could run it multiple times on one pod and all my coffee tasted like plastic for a month, if they can't understand where you're at then they won't end up where you're going, I can't wait for right now

☻

I CAN'T WAIT FOR RIGHT NOW

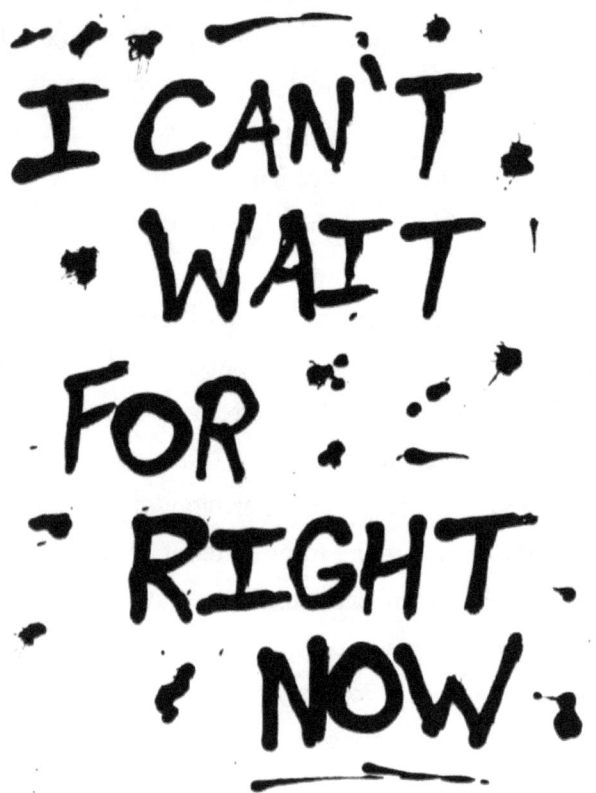

DAGGERS

One of my cats seems to run towards loud noises while the other one cowers in fear, stay if you want to stay, there will come a point in the river of your life where all spills out into a great body of water but right now we're stuck in the rapids, it is time to take the cast off my broken soul and let it gain its strength back, the ritual of a brand new day, how will you integrate your new ways of thinking, an old perfectly worn in catcher's mitt, a much needed vacation, I'm ready to stake myself to my art and see where it drags me, I wonder what times my friends remember but I forget, try to avoid counting the blank pages, I remember a few times coming in completely under prepared and just barely making it through so I prepare a little bit now, doing hard things you don't really want to do will prepare you for the hard things that you are eventually forced to do, just beneath my ever present anxiety is an extremely optimistic outlook, good intentions are the best pathway to good outcomes, I would rather be naïve than be a cynical prick, I would not be surprised if you found success doing the exact opposite of whatever I tell you, my worries come from a basic fear for survival but my goals are the whole point of surviving, if you are coming from an honest place and your steps are true you will never lose your driving force, I would have got in trouble if I showed the emotion that I was feeling, believe in the ones who believe in themselves, crying in the back of the car, either achieve your dreams or allow your outlook to be seen as delusional to everyone in your life, your local submersible dealership, I've still never been in a hot air balloon, if you're okay with not getting your results all at once you're going to be fine, I want to be able to feel momentarily sad and not let it ruin me, finishing a good book on a rainy afternoon, don't let us forget to get a group picture, I wish you knew how much I miss you, what in your life would you lose your life for, one or two really good decisions will determine the rest of our lives, I will leave my outcome up to the air I breathe and the sleep that I get each night, take the phone off the hook and talk with me deep into the night, factually inaccurate but sure feels nice, taste the music, let it knock out all your teeth, a closet dedicated to costumes, planning our next decade, phasing in and out of reality just to blame our attention spans, I'm putting genuine effort into what might look like garbage to an outsider but hopefully makes sense to someone who knows what they are looking for, my goal is a psychedelic experience through words, have you ever stopped and thought about the fact that we're basically mud just held together by static electricity, I think I'm done playing dumb, I am working to pay back every cent of my psychic debt, remember I'm just trying to make you think, look up your heroes starting point, help others feel better, I would like to stop thinking about myself entirely at some point, there is a part of me that has felt safe creating artwork since I was a little kid but my fear of judgment has challenged that safety, mystery is necessary despite how desperately we crave answers, when looking at the stars from laying on the moon the Earth is beautifully in view, one degree closer to the truth, the screen time app is devastating, they released an acoustic version of my favorite album, that voice hasn't been heard in a long time, I can already feel myself forgetting a lot of the context behind many of these lines that I'm writing and that is just going to have to be fine, my instincts tell me there is no correct answer, imagine if we scientifically determine that all of this has just been a whale's weird dream after eating the wrong kind of fish, why couldn't it be me, I have little to base this on but I'm assuming the paparazzi are a weird group of people, a nineties sit-com where an NSA employee and a watercolor painter end up as roommates and are forced to learn about themselves and the deep state in a wholesome way, just wait until they invent self-driving motorcycles, who tested all the bungee jumping equipment first, donuts for breakfast every morning, the freshest air you'll ever breathe, you can see the meaning or you can strip it all away, senseless violence seems irreconcilable regardless of which worldview you contort it through, exercising a neurological process, like you wouldn't believe, blooming of any sort, I'm listening to all my hopeful feelings and working on calming all the feelings that keep disagreeing with the hopeful ones, convenient syzygies, midnight full moon canoe excursion, if I were not a seeker I'm sure I would be a wanderer because I really don't want to stop moving, you never know, I would like to take the blue sky with me but I know it has to come and go with the wind, the roof caved in and the firefighters ran right in, farming a field of only flowers, allow the moment its moment, he really thought he had something here, the most fantastical imaginings originating in a human brain, the amount of beauty on this water droplet we're stuck on is astounding, cliffs made of salt and islands of ice, our cities smell like humans, the most comfortable bed I'll ever lay in, desolation can be awe inspiring too, if I'm lucky I'll get to walk in some of the places our ancestors considered holy before they are all gone, you don't have to be brilliant to still be considered a thinker, when I say 'I' let it mean 'you' and when I say 'you' let it mean 'I', all the time in the desert to forget that there is an ocean or all the time in the city to forget that there is a place where you can feel completely and utterly alone, you won't know what you are capable of until you attempt to do what you think you are incapable of but want to do anyway, was it a juxtaposition or just a comparison, when human relations are suffering this badly it becomes difficult to get people to care about the natural world, your companionship is all that matters to me now, the planets shine like stars in the night sky too, I love when someone makes me think so I would like to try and return the favor, resolve your darkest aspect so they are just shadows instead of pitch black with their own gravitational pull, I don't know if we have anything modern that will last as long as how long the ancient world has lasted, I have seen a turtle and a bald eagle in the same lifetime, as long as I'm alive I might as well keep carving these squiggles into these rocks, can you take a kayak through the canals in Venice, for each promise I've failed to keep I will try to make two to hold forever, I can sort of feel that I'm on a planet even though I've never been to space, the sheer amount that there is to see basically guarantees we will see something amazing, I hope to look up at Petra one day and wonder how they ever carved such a thing, if only I could overcome all these goddamn weaknesses, can't we take a second to just appreciate where we're at, I don't love how technological devices are encroaching on time we previously dedicated to daydreaming, no matter how long I look at them the pyramids at Giza will never not be unbelievable, I'll use double and triple negatives if I want to fuck you, awe and wonder are proven to be beneficial to your mental health, my primary sources are obvious observations, have you ever found out that you actually have exactly what it takes, what have we done to the Elephants and the Whales, it feels safe to assume that what is natural is also good, at some point or another I might be called mentally unwell but I would like to formally deny that claim right here right now, we need to treat those suffering from mental illness better, I wish I could sleep as good as my cats, close your eyes and imagine you are a sheep running with your herd across the greenest pastures you've ever seen, calm deep breaths either deep underwater or standing on the moon, it's hard to know how a tree feels but I would bet my last dollar that it feels good, what do you look for in a friendship, what do you consider magnificent, there is path through the woods that no human will ever walk again and it's being reclaimed by the forest, my belly is full I should be able to tackle whatever the universe needs me to do at the time, are you able to let your mind wander without following it into a dark place, this is all I currently have, I can just tell our lives are all a grand spiritual lesson of some kind, use these jumbled words and ideas however you wish, they are trying to rebuild the fourth wall as we speak but we will not let up our attack, the food is ready, I feel like if you are truly cursed you should get at least one elaborate puzzle to complete for a chance to lift the curse, if you are a young person reading this you should spend the next ten years getting really into wing suit base jumping and film all of it from the first person point of view and post it on YouTube for people like me to watch, I wonder what I haven't considered at all that is still definitely going to happen, I want both the curiosity of a kitten and the patience of a glacier, the laws of human existence and perception maintain that tomorrow will stay an absolute and total mystery, it is much easier to gamble your life savings away when you don't have a life savings, I feel like my snap judgments are frequently and almost reliably wrong, do I even have a badge of honor, a person will take you in when you feel most alone, psychologists still don't know why we dream and yet they pretend to tell me how we think, my friend told me that when we die we appear in a giant movie theater with all our best friends with a universally powerful remote control that can play back all the funniest times that anyone can think of, please just hear me out, I know as little as you do but maybe if we trade our stupid theories we can come up with a little bit of truth, begging and pleading for the question, its depressing to think the lines are already drawn for the next world war, do any of us even have a shred of a chance or is it all an illusion, if I were a weather system would I be a drought or a monsoon, hours and hours of work on the back end, no one loves the moocher, I'll detach from judgement for fear of harsh judgment but reattach at the slightest positivity, wresting with an attempt to be honest, my eyes hurt for what I don't even know I'm looking for, you can disagree with the great philosophers they're all dead, high praise all the way from the bottom, people watching as their lives slip by, learning about yourself through making a decision you'll hate for the rest of your life, there are things I said in elementary school that still bother me, occasionally you'll have to at least try to be the bigger person, the analysis of a lucky break, am I supposed to be angry at the state of world politics or am I supposed to reach a conclusion that I can only impact my immediate surroundings, I believe many of the most mind shattering thought patterns are presented in such a dry way that people don't pay attention to them, it can go from obvious to making no sense too damn fast, I feel like the vast number of interpretations of what God even is somehow points to God's existence, you have to be willing and able to heal, I have trouble understanding the stylistic choice of a sweater vest, I am very lucky to have developed the friendships that I have in my lifetime, success is accessible, I need a buzzword dictionary, have your assumptions ever been true, bring your goals up to a boil, retreat back to the nonsensical, can you practice abstract thought, I have trouble recognizing any rationality in our current existence besides the regular rising and setting of the sun, I wanted to be an inventor but I'm no engineer so where does that leave me, the smallest aspect is as integral to the whole as the massive support beam, prove your worth, I would love to forgive myself but we can't always get what we want can we, don't fret unless you're a guitarist, vibrant red and blue face paint, to what extent can we really be free, can you sum up the universe in seven sentences, school is unfortunately a subpar teacher no offense to teachers, I've been feeling like I have a chance lately, you're a good person and you're worth it, sailing right into a hurricane, I would like to get so far along the road of progress that I couldn't stop myself even if I tried, it can be extremely difficult to realize you've been holding yourself back, it is not a bad thing to agree that there is more to life than this, I couldn't even wager a guess what'll happen next, a well-placed contraction or abbreviation can perfect the flow of a sentence, I could use some handwriting lessons, it's just me, the place where a mountain is your father and the ocean is your mother and the trees and the flowers are your brothers and sisters, was I born with an ultimate goal in mind, I'll eat just about anything that was pan fried in crushed potato chips, the variety of possible games is infinite on its own but then we can take out all the rules and winners and losers, elevate your possible end point, I want to remain in the state where I wake up and fall deep into what I feel like I'm meant to be doing, I already wonder what it's like living in the ocean and I'm not even taking into account the vast difference between a whale and a spider crab, it's good when you lose track of time and you're late but you're alongside the person who made you forget about the clock in the first place, there are many factors that could go wrong in the healing process, if you like this wait until you read my stuff that actually makes sense, she brought me coffee in the morning, he had a way of talking that would always leave you trying to guess the next word, if I were to leave this room a little too soon I would have vastly different thoughts in my future, spread my ashes at a library, it is strange knowing how flawed our memories are, why don't you do what is completely out of character for you and see if you surprisingly like it, encouragement is different from egging on, stop fiddling with the pages and write goddamn it, snowflakes don't taste like anything but we love catching them on our tongue, if I've found people who wanted to help me you'll find people who want to help you, my kitten attacked my feet as viscously as it could, is there some grand understanding or do we just die with all the same questions, do what makes you lose track of time for hours for a few decades, commit to what you're doing, if you don't dance go dance once before you can't, graduate level panic, synonyms and antonyms for existential dread, original enough, a photo copy of a mentally ill person's hand written schematics of a time machine fell in the wrong hands, I feel like I have a hint of what it takes and the rest of it will be luck, surprise yourself, be gentle on you, I don't fully understand my own desired outcomes, I don't know if there are unlimited things to say but there are certainly unlimited ways to say them, I started drinking cappuccinos around age twenty seven, take a blowtorch to ignorance, I would like an ultra-terrestrial intelligent being to go have a conversation with me somewhere in my past, I would like to continue having fun with my thoughts, we're in a speeding car with a driver who doesn't quite know the curves in the road, stop hiding your feelings, do you really know how to contemplate infinity, I wonder if I will ever see the north or the south pole, reverse savagery, I want to hear you tell the tales that no one has ever heard before, make sure everyone else around you is still alive, I count myself lucky that I've never fallen down a crevasse while skiing, we're selling all our belongings if anyone is interested, please support your local whatever, I accidentally bought a cruise ship on E-bay last night, you don't have to keep beating yourself up like that, what exactly does chemically balanced even look like, get as close as you possibly can, I want your dream to come true for you too, not all life experience is good life experience, please include me in your next scheme, the plot to climb the hoover dam, the federal government wants to ban all fun, I wish there was an elaborate scavenger hunt hidden within this book but there is not, use your damn eyeballs, adopt a kitten, we've come much further than we even intended originally, telegraph your punch and get knocked out, not everyone is going to agree with you but you really don't need them to, at some point I decided I was going to use words as my weapon, just a little bit better is always attainable, collect all the memories your brain can possibly remember, do you ever freak out about what is going to happen next, if we don't cross paths in this life I will be sure to look for you in the next one, they wouldn't publish this book so I did it myself, I feel like it is just as crazy to believe the position of the stars does not affect us at all as it is to believe that they dictate your entire life, embellished verbatim, no one is prioritizing being cool to one another anymore, if you're trying to measure my politics just assume I'm against you and we'll go from there, success is just around the bend, I'm sick of being blamed for shit I had no part of, the transition from enduring painful loneliness to enjoying peaceful solitude is truly wonderful, want to enroll in some classes with me, if you are just starting out college look into CLEP and DSST exams, I realize this text might make me look crazy but I promise I'm not anymore, scientists made the shocking discovery that the universe is made up of a trillion words of poetry, the living embodiment of doing whatever the fuck you want, you are unlimited but you just don't know it yet, I hope you are able to see through my bullshit, I want to go snorkeling more often, imagine being a horse and just galloping, some of us forget the heroes journey when we get stuck in the nine to five, I like to think that my ideas are weird enough to be unique, not guilty your honor, we cancelled our plans and watched a movie instead, if they don't like you it is their loss, you can't say I'm not doing my own thing, counteract the technology brain rot by reading books and writing thousands of words, instead of writing this book I could have like fifty thousand tweets but oh well here we are, I've grown just through knowing you, all I want to do is finish this page, being able to do what you want is an absolute blessing, fresh cherries in the fridge, I'm tired of having a long way to go, I have no idea what my cat is meowing about, the wildest claims you've ever heard, I hope we get a chance to catch up soon, quick before we're all gone, I hate forgetting my ideas, I had a feeling there was more coming, it is pretty obvious when you are holding back, I want ice cream every night around midnight, my ultimate goal will be to communicate the lessons of a post-scarcity society, it is pretty clear that humans are currently not working with a mutual goal in mind, I'm fully hydrated today, are you going to be shocked how your life turns out or will it all finally make sense, not all of us will get a chance to face our fears so it is an honor for you to be facing yours, societies do tend to crumble so we should probably care for ours a little more while we still have one, why am I hearing police sirens in my small town, it's okay to be needy as long as you're aware of it and communicate those needs fairly, if I can't trust myself I'll just trust the passage of time, the turning point within the self where we finally stick up for it, my best friend looked at me and said consider it done no questions asked, what do you now take for granted that you used to want so badly, we were put here to think and we don't even want to anymore, crawling down a chimney is wild behavior, keep chirping, at this point just wanting to get by feels like wanting to be a millionaire, the military uses dolphins for underwater warfare, I regret not trash talking more when I played organized sports, who taught you that, go where your interest takes you before we run out of time, chasing the feeling of I never quite thought of it that way, I don't want your sympathy get it away from me but empathy is pretty chill though, someone has masturbated while thinking about you in the most flattering way possible, we can create a fictional city in our mind and fill it with hundreds of fictional characters and we care for them like we care for anyone else in our lives, shatter all your teeth off your rock bottom and then get back up, I want to be someone building you up and encouraging you because so few in our world do, once you start throwing numbers around and start adding and subtracting I've probably already lost you, ask the person closest to you to fulfill their vision, make every step in your life a step towards being better, if you're not amazed by the miracle of life you might want to surround yourself with a few more interesting people, be an interesting prism for the light to pour through in a way it never refracted before, derive your self worth from a healthy place, chasing pennies when there are trillions being passed around, what is worth your complete exhaustion, the most you of you, my mouth watered like I was going to vomit from sheer panic, I go outside at night when the sky is clear and I try to jump off the Earth and into space, walk your soul right up and out of your body, scratching through concrete with only fingernails and will power, the powerful urge to set sail in an old wooden ship, as exciting as going from the shallow to the deep end when you were just a little kid, nothing is worse than the ones who just blindly listen to the order givers and the nay sayers, you will not have to grow too old for your childhood to have taken place in a historical moment, I've lost myself before and finding myself again was the best part of my life, we're better off enjoying the pleasures while they float by than waiting and waiting for ones that may never come, if talking is a product I'll be a rambling millionaire, my throat catches often so I have to practice breathing, think how far it is possible to go, accept the care of the universe, what happened to the atoms that were in our bodies just a few years ago, I saw that man drink gasoline, trust that the next few seconds will go as planned, I hope you sleep well tonight, unconditional certified back up, all those lessons in all those fantasy books were all drawn from real life experience, what is true for your hero is true for you too, I want my work to be toward my own furthering, all this time to just now notice the hole in my pocket, I'm not good with mental math but I do offer other mental states like mental gymnastics or mental illness, I paid a guy to plumb down into my subconscious and clean the dust off the shelves so we'll see what he reports back whenever he finishes, I really don't like how the phone works like a slot machine now, have you ever stumbled into definitely not your crowd and had to stumble back out, no matter what way I try to look at it we seem to be a small part of a much larger whole, it would be so cool if there is an elaborate afterlife and we are in a training ground, are you passing the tests that life is giving you, my own head says some of the nastiest shit about me, close the door on your way out, I'm excited to bump into you in my future, I had to yell at my cat to get it to stop attacking the skier on my television, I'm sorry if I didn't deliver what I promised, unlock your mental handcuffs or at least admit you're wearing them, mentality determines the rest, french kiss it, death to the copy pasters, all my life they told me to lose the attitude but it turns out I've really needed this attitude, for once I'm comfy in my own skin, I want a functional space suit just in case, move until you're excited by your prospects, research delayed gratification, it is respectable to take the bits that apply to you, whole new outfit, when is the last time you felt like you were floating, longevity and security to all, find rushing water and contemplate the power of time as expressed through erosion, if there are too many holes in the foundation eventually we will lose the building, learn the principles and execute them to the best of your ability, perfect lighting, a sunrise I'll never forget, our pain can't be our only motivator, a chrome pencil, more oil for the furnace, the great bouncy house war of two thousand and four, never quit playing wiffle ball, humans create good no matter what bad we're surrounded by, we need to treat teachers better, we found the closest parking spot we could ask for, pages missing in my owners manual, there are many imaginary lines that have been drawn but oftentimes if you find the place in the real world there is literally nothing there, try to fail once in a while, a correct glasses prescription can change how you see everything, we're placed in a world with killing on every level and told specifically to never murder anyone, I want to get heavily into fencing in my forties in case lightsabers get invented or I fall into a time portal and have to live the rest of my life as a knight or a samurai, what were the atomic level secrets of the iron age, what if dolphins are so smart that they know exactly what happens when you start messing around with technology and that's the only reason they don't use any, breakneck speeds, I caught a leprechaun when I was a kid and he granted all my wishes and I'm actually just living them out right now, I don't know if I'll get a chance to be chivalrous but I hope I rise to the occasion, a cool demeanor until it is revealed to be oblivious, beware the snake oil salesmen from the eighteen hundreds are alive and well on TikTok and Instagram, pick the lockbox of secrets, there is immense mental wellness power in repeated acts of gratitude, fireworks must have been so incredibly cool when they were first invented in ancient China, you are fatigued but you are going to keep going, why are our schools of thought leading us into violence so reliably, if you are going to speak ensure the words you are using are worth saying, we easily forget that another name for our moment in history is the Long Peace however it might be nearing its end, I can't believe lions are so closely related to this blob of sleeping fur on my couch, how far into disfavor have I already fallen, when was my last incredible month, thank god for every healthy relationship, I'm sorry I tend to withdraw when I am depressed, cyber humiliation is an objectively horrific philosophical nightmare, don't forget there have been no coronations in America, burn all the itchy blankets, we're really going to regret all this plastic, I don't know much about trees but oak just sounds like such a good lumber, who will be mad about the way I choose to spell baloney, would we have to change how we live if we found out every cell in our bodies is a conscious being, a clean pair off pants that fit perfectly, if all has been determined I have a problem with the current arrangement, please just be anti-authoritarian, how long will bicycles exist into the future, arguing about which Pixar film is the best for three hours with your friend on the phone, I feel like not enough kids want to become astronauts these days, buy a truck or a cool van, you can never go wrong with a quesadilla, exercise your patience, I never had a teacher mention the importance of a virtuous life in my entire four years of high school, a hot shower for every person on Earth, there is a vacant city that the whole area once thought was crucial to society, are you currently in pursuit of a noble cause, we may never fully know the operation of our soul but we can certainly feel our spirit, we should cure every allergy, the simple potato has saved countless numbers from hunger, can we have leaders who are in agreement for just five or ten years, do people understand that the library has FREE stuff, the air I'm breathing tells me the universe is trying to help us on some level, the luminous is becoming trivial, a friendly discourse with your arch nemesis, we are all taking part in a hand me down system of knowledge reaching us distorted through time like an elaborate game of telephone despite the fact that we have a device in our pocket that can answer the majority of reasonable questions that we can currently think of, why aren't there thirteen months in the year, who the hell has been poking all the bears that need this warning, you will be faced with self-doubt whether you are at your very beginning or the pinnacle of your success, are you physically or spiritually drained, I loved her from the soles of her feet up through her heart and all the way back down through her fingertips, once you start following yourself you'll always find yourself in brand new places, many of us have lost our previously natural and intuitive ability to forage for food in the forest, what inhibitions do I have that are quite literally holding me back, maintain and appreciate the smallest bits of your life that are making you happy, a large iced coffee with frozen coffee cubes and free refills, I feel like there is an obvious connection between the nucleus of an atom and the nucleus of a cell and the human brain and the core of the Earth and the sun and the center of our galaxy, all we can do from here is continue, I want to meet the crazy motherfucker who invented the kaleidoscope, my grammar won't be perfect but I'm doing my best, there was a vague outline on my kitchen floor that told me that someone had been there just before, a two car garage filled with survival tools to save our entire neighborhood during the end of the world, how often should we be forgiving the same person, Boston traffic merges when it wants to, are microbes acting solely via the chemical laws of nature or do they have some agency in where they float to next, it isn't feeling very festive in here, why do we respond so well to rhythm but animals don't seem to be affected at all, you can have the last bite, the loudest noise you'll ever hear, what would the adorable gerbil think of our invention of rat poison, experience as a function of time multiplied by the number of endeavors tried, accepting the lessons and teachings that have endured for thousands of years, what from today will last through history, chase the feeling of learning what you never could have possibly guessed, appreciation of the minutia, I'm no longer aggravated, beware the danger of fast forwarding to the good parts, embrace differences as they arise, hopefully our great-great-great grandchildren are very familiar with the space walk, the mythology and folklore of the UFO following us into our space-faring years as we continue to find no sign of life anywhere outside of our planet for millenia, accept the harshest lessons, referencing felonies in a poetry book, lay in the sunshine, reality is going to disintegrate too just like our dead bodies, I don't know if I've ever really had a field day with my ideas, they told us to keep our mouths shut and the true tragedy is that we listened, the smallest gesture could mean the world, it won't make any sense until we're standing at the podium, light as many spiritual fires as you have matches for, we could be dreaming a lot longer than we remember, say cheese for the ghosts and spirits that are watching you now, I don't care what the technologists say the virtual will never compete with what is both good and real, I feel for the people who truly have no one else in their corner fighting their battles with them, never forget the people who back you up, the thought crimes have already been committed now we must serve our sentence, do it differently like you said you would, I'm asking you to look deeply and find the meaning where you see fit, some people don't realize that making changes requires you to really change, we can all fly but we just really enjoy the ground, the food on your plate was manifested from heaven, the ones who understand violence are typically the very last to call for violence, why is it so easy to take it all for granted, the miracle of eyesight, has the axis of evil always known what it was, give me the weirdest hypothesis you can think of, a hot meal, ruining your whole day by thinking of all the disasters that probably won't even happen, you want to be neither the guy at the bar every single night or the guy who has never set foot in a dive bar, pain in the side from laughter, stealing interstate signs off the highway, the fulfillment felt from feeding and taking care of a pet, I feel like the dictionary is way too short for what it is supposed to be, the privilege of continued existence, be the type of friend that you need, ten pounds of raw material, we saw that while we were outside, if there is absolutely no purpose for all this suffering I really do have a bone to pick with God, be a good host give extra blankets and pillows, strive to become a society that no longer needs welfare and everyone just has what they need, value size tub of ranch dressing, when the drain that has been clogged for months finally flows perfectly, find some way to benefit yourself and others, acceptance can be really hard to come by these days, we see bundles of joy way more often than bundles of regret and sorrow, scrape your hands raw from the effort, we need to treat our veterans better, try your absolute best not to throw any bricks through any windows, the endless groan emanating from the internal pain of regret, what will be found during the archeological expedition into your psyche, we all say divide and conquer all the time and yet we still just easily and willingly divide ourselves, I don't know if there is any order in the chaos but it would appear there is at least occasional meaning, burn yourself out struggling for years over a good thing, listen to those who are calling on you, if your quads are tired you're on the uphill, I bet there is life all throughout the Milky Way never mind the entire universe, that moment the animal in your house approaches you and curls up next to you fully on their own accord, there was talk at the coffee shop this morning of planted seeds and sunlight and growth but I couldn't quite hear all the words they were saying as they sipped their beverages, there is nothing wrong with emulating your heroes but eventually you want to be totally and wholly you, some crop circles truly have absolutely no explanation and no one claiming that they did it, look up China's underground Great Wall, people who go from extremely lonely to completely comfortable in solitude tend to be quite interesting because they found what was interesting about themselves, its okay to understand that the grass is always greener on the other side but that doesn't mean you should never take a calculated leap towards a better life, it's okay to wait for a lucky break as long as you're doing everything you possibly can to increase your odds, honestly if you make me laugh I can forgive just about anything, he even walked with confidence, maybe I don't actually exist, once we start debating which is base reality we will know for sure that it isn't ours, we should probably have a massive nerf war to settle this, if magic is real I will accidentally write a spell eventually, there is little purpose in seeing the entire world without having someone along with you or having someone close to tell the whole story to when you finally get home unless you have some deep level of individual spiritual enlightenment I guess, frequently the worst part of a moment is the one you are most thankful for in the future, just vibrate, I will leave the world with a piece of my mind, a psychedelic trip worth of information on a device in your pocket, the question is whether we are headed toward a better life or not, expand what you know, drink from the cup with the tea leaves, move the wooden blocks with your mind, what do you think of first when I tell you to start living your life, an aspect of life which has not yet begun for you, broken paw, perfect alignment, an empty shopping cart in the bushes, what will happen next if we fail to rise to the occasion, do not harbor your resentments cut their mooring lines and release them into the storm, just stick to any semblance of a plan, a brand new way of being, earn your future, I'll never forget these past three years and I'll probably be able to say that for every point in my life, watch the world around you or take part in changing the world around you, a life worth every second of living by the end of it, we were stuck in the snow for hours with just a spot of liquor, planning your radical change is different from executing it, cut out your behaviors that are harming you, nightmares are strangely safe because eventually you are scared awake, learn as many memory tricks and strategies that you can, we all think we're ready, be the evidence you need when it is time to believe in yourself, I just want to introduce you to the possibility of feeling better, it is extremely flawed logic for someone to hate you for something as arbitrary as a worldview or as impossible to change as your hair or skin color, there is no point in writing without honesty, I have never felt represented by any political candidate that has appeared on my TV, be the unlikely scenario, how many millionaires had to couch surf at some point, we are building islands now, what will remain of humanity in the next phase of the human's evolution, once you finally get the ball rolling make sure you keep it rolling, do you know the myths well enough to apply the lessons, listen to the warnings because you may only get one or two, you will show what you are capable of by what you push yourself to do, did you ever end up finding your wheel house, I saw you skip a milestone what was that about, I would accept partial credit at this point, how to change your life in ten days, my dog had a long day, the danger of an entire life doing everything you're supposed to do and have absolutely nothing to show for it, take more from behind your eyes and behind your heart and give it to the first person you see, fever dream journal, all this talk about psychedelics when deliriants grow on the side of the road, I still want a bright future, I like people with strange beliefs, you'll get very good at shaking off the doubt but there will be times that even you think it might take you down, will I ever be able to replicate a feeling perfectly through writing, I would bet humans only know a thousandth of a fraction of a percentage of what there is to know but our advantage is that we're able to learn, I try not to take my first shit of the day until eleven AM because that is when my phone's screen time blocker unlocks, you should be happy when you are finally faced with a brand new set of problems, whatever ends up actually happening can be vastly better than some lofty fantasy when you learn to appreciate the current second, the common worldwide practice of selling yourself short, you do not have to let your mistakes define your character, I have a goal not a dream or fantasy, not many people learn how much whatever it takes actually weighs, these little imaginary critters seem to like me, unfortunately it can be impossibly hard to really tell how close you are to your own goals, a terrible thing about the internet is that you cannot properly size up who is attacking you, I can feel my desires slowly ceasing their domination of my life it's called going with the flow, going through the act of not quitting, study what interests you most, I don't really want to play for any of the teams that I see playing, I swam as deep as I could and I refuse to come back empty handed, one of the most brutally sad things to learn in life is that not everyone recovers, you're falling through space in an armored pod at terminal velocity to explode onto the surface of a planet you've never been to, spiritual truths are not riddles, being who you are meant to be is a verb not a noun or a process not a conclusion, which piece of art or music made you cry, you can engage with the world in ways that other people assume is impossible, with a single step missing from a thousand mile journey you will not arrive, it will engulf you like ball lightening, when your truth goes against another's the shared goal should be to understand each other's, do what you came here to do, I need a quiet place to throw paint at a wall for a few hours, the second that I put the pen down I feel like I'm slacking off, it took a long time to find anything resembling self confidence inside of me, you may feel protected but the chinks in your armor are obvious to someone out there, part of me is a little bit scared of the good or bad that I might be capable of, as close to a regular person as I will ever feel, the teachings all seem to say struggle is good so I don't know, surround sound death metal lullaby, all my best homies have tinnitus, there is something my parents don't know about their own kitchen, oftentimes teenagers hear what is supposed to be a deterrent as encouragement and I was one of those teenagers, if you are growing plants or painting paintings or writing computer code you are bringing something into existence that was not here just a minute ago and I truly believe that is exactly what we are all here for, I feel like run on sentences get a bad rap, at some point you'll realize how much you've been holding back, keep planting seeds no matter the weather, I love your flaws, don't you get it I can't live for any other reason, just because the whole world is against you doesn't mean you have to be against yourself too, greatness has never once happened overnight, learn strategies to get yourself thinking, a slice of blueberry pie, not a single person took the same path as you but every single person had to continue along their own to get where they wanted to go, people with a lifetime of saying the wrong thing especially know how to say the right thing when it finally counts, I will succeed, the truth is often unacceptable, beat yourself up just long enough to toughen up, thankful for the many chances that I've been given, if you take the moral path it may be a slower and steadier trip but it will include better companions and a better destination, endless beverages in the fridge, praise all the broken brains that keep thinking anyway, teach yourself not to be guided by your impulses leaving nothing but your convictions to guide your decisions, it really just makes perfect sense that you want more when not appreciating what you already have, are we being held to a beneficial moral standard, I'm trying to stop pontificating, do you ever stumble across another mass scale evil being perpetrated and think how the hell is all this shit still going on, I'm sorry if no one has come along to tell you you're doing okay, I like being where the seasons change but I wonder how I would feel with sunshine every day, pray for the lost, I don't miss who you were before, it can very often be summed up in just one word but sometimes it's just fun to elaborate, the dunce cap never really came back into style, my brother is a good man, lately I've come across a few people who believe in my dream with me, you have to think that it might be your perfect time in life, I would like to try to understand what we used to say was impossible to understand, I won't call myself stupid and give up on a subject, why were we all brought up with a constant feeling that we had done something wrong, it can be fuzzy from afar but up close it is crystal clear, don't try to keep them, I would like to just sit and think all day but our society isn't exactly set up that way, Americans think we are the world when we are such a small fraction of humanity, beg your leaders to at least postpone the wars, unanswered questions from the molecules all the way up to the multiverse, I yearn painfully and then jolt myself out of it by looking around at how good my life already is, cool crisp thoughts, remember how that day ended, of course it is easy to feel lost look how big the universe is, the froth at the top of freshly made espresso, who can I reach, buy a broken dirt bike on Facebook marketplace and fix it up over the summer, I hope your headache was worth all those thoughts, there are a few words that I try not to throw around and that is one of them, be careful saying could when you should be saying will, I've breathed thin air and choked on salt water, go if you want to go, our back burner is getting crowded, it has never been yours, I didn't have to swear, it was safe there, there are many stories about the faith of sheep, fields upon fields of your favorite crop, to be holy in the least holy of places, there is an underworld beneath wherever you're standing, I trust what my situation brings, achieve terminal velocity for your soul, it would be fascinating if we achieve even a resemblance of eternal life, watch your head as you fall, I hope to never need to use one of those safety cards they put in the back of airplane seats, it can be both extremely easy and impossibly difficult, I am still me, I wish there were no language barriers, it is a magnificent feeling finishing what you started, the concepts that I repeat over and over will have to be my guiding principles, watch as eternity ensues with or without us, what is stuck in the two dimensional that belongs up in the seventh or eighth, if you can't see the greater picture then telling you it's right in front of you won't even help, they'll have to recategorize fungus to be its only biological entity pretty soon, we think we're so much better than the animals but we can't think like them either, some knowledge is unavoidable, nearly choking to death from laughter as a kid, the sound of the wind at high altitude, we may have every shoreline mapped but I've never sailed to any of them, if you can acknowledge that there are different ways of living then we can be friends, snap judgments are tiring and unhelpful, if a computer can build a consciousness then what about the exact same programming made out of massive mechanical gears, occupy your space, every question has already been asked but I don't think you can say the same for every answer, we are so worried about computers gaining sentience when we seem to be valuing our own sentience less than ever, apparently I have a lot to say and I've allowed myself to believe that it's okay to say it, I hope you're doing well, if I was thinking this wasn't worth it the entire time I probably would have played a lot more videogames, know when to double down and when to back out, when you see how they've failed in teaching us it'll make you angry learning what is out there to learn, I'm terrified of the brain chips, I hope all the arcades stay, there is so much that I wish would happen that will probably never, you are always welcome to try, I distinctly remember finding a guy on the internet that was mailing dreams to people, a part of me deeply respects the old rituals and part of me is scared that I've never been on a spirit walk, now I think it's safe to say that I've paid my dues, stitch me up doc, those conversations you have with your tattoo artist, part of me really wants to earn it, we all want it easy but a few of us know how bad that would really be, what arbitrary constraints are you holding yourself to on account of someone else, I love the weirdos, your skin feels so good after falling through the mist of a cloud, spaghetti and meatballs with garlic bread when you're hungry, I feel like many people want to go to outer space and very few people want to explore the bottom of the ocean, you are stumbling down a dark tunnel but every so often there is a light, love a good who done it, look at all that we've survived, standing at the edge of madness and getting luckily pulled back, resist the urge to put your brain on auto pilot, ice cold pond water, make the needed repairs, waltz on through, let this be your message to be yourself, we are massively under-utilizing the human potential, I feel like there are multiple types of building blocks for life, we are the sparkle from the sunlight hitting the water, most of us are just trying to have a good time and get by, let your life live, from rough waters to smooth sailing, oftentimes we shut down because activation requires acknowledgment of all we have to change, move with intent, prompt your needed actions, a style which is difficult to define, instigating fights with your friends, throw the etiquette in the trash, how many different ways can I say be yourself, bumping into who you're next to when you're totally lost on where you should be going, at some point you may have to walk through coals, I hope they find me waiting here, I'm sorry for those who were forced to be vicious, we are all born with the same questions but are free to answer in as unique a way as we would like to live, we think we're better than the ocean just because we float on top of it, I've not always been this positive, the combination of chaos and order, we have a strange ability to describe that which we can't even completely understand, I'm not a big umbrella guy, I might not be ready yet, we should build a spiral railroad extending into low Earth orbit, of course the dreamers are in charge of the dreamscape, each of us tries to hold a corner of reality in place, always take the spiritual agreement that promises eternity because it is always enough time, I do not give permission to any government or corporate entity to use my likeness via computer generation of any kind when I'm dead and gone, what if there is a real Nigerian prince that needs help by mail, will conformity end when individuality becomes the goal of all the conformists, you can probably tell I'm not exactly up to date on most subjects, stick your chin out in defiance, my organs are currently doing their jobs, we've been duped and now we have to recover, I would do some nude modeling for fine art if my girlfriend allowed it, there is no map of the required steps to becoming free, I would not be surprised at all to find an extraterrestrial institution keeping its eye on us funny little humans and making adjustments when absolutely necessary, what can we withstand, at long last might be just another moment or two away, the boundaries are often an illusion that will break when we pass through them, are you your own opponent or teammate, gross negligence of the psyche, at this point I would love to see what a bull actually does to a china shop, we're looking for the way in our sleep instead of waking, no one has ever dug down deep into themselves and uncovered absolutely nothing, twelve dynamic duos in direct competition, the farthest distance that I've ever seen, when I was a kid

I really thought we would have hover cars by the twenty twenties, fill the gaps, her handwriting was astounding, I hope I don't crush like a styrofoam cup under all the pressure, if it's possible to harm your brain with your thinking then it stands to reason you can also strengthen it, we're building a ramp to jump the fourth wall are you in, I wish I had a great evil to fight in a mystical realm type of way, interdimensional elevator ride, inactivity always makes it worse, when your hands are caked in dirt we have hot water and soap, I'm not coming down, I had pretty intense psychosis but I sort of road it out, getting our minds right should always be priority one, if you are already saying it won't work too early you are just trying to end the uncertainty but really you should feel excited by uncertainty because it implies you still have possibilities, we explore the world to find ourselves and we look within ourselves to better understand the world, of course you have the answer you're the one who asked the question, I walked a little closer to my goal today, an infectious way of looking at the world, do not go your whole life without trying something unprecedented, we're not lost in the woods necessarily we've just been coming across a shocking number of criss crossing paths, I finally woke up and started doing what I'm actually meant to, font size can make all the difference, cool on the approach, it's totally okay to look like a fool, roller skating to funk, you're seeing patterns that I'm not seeing and I'm seeing patterns that you're not seeing, I can tell that there is more substance here than there was before, turn it into an adventure, we are laying the concrete for the foundation now, the desert opened up ahead of us as wide as the sea we just came from, we won't even know which plants to eat when we land on that planet, there were no friendlies that we could find, I broke all twenty of my fingers and toes but I still didn't let go, cybernetic eye socket, working with reality rather than against it, even free standing structures seem to fall on their own, I feel relief, when you couldn't have thought of a better way to say it, I've been proud of the work that I've been doing lately, we're supposed to be having fun, don't ask for more right after receiving, what is it for you that will just never get old, what is life without flying a couple kites in a couple lightening storms, start with your favorite, greetings from the past of another dimension, if you're reading this please help, I wonder if I'll end up taking any secrets to my grave, do what works for you, I'm so glad I grew up with a trampoline, there are slow parts of the river and there are rapids, I would like to find out what they want no one knowing, I would be nowhere without strong coffee, freedom within constraints with the possibility of a breakthrough, you'll really know you are here for a reason when you narrowly avoid death, the world is filled with heroes, even if the same pattern was repeated twice it is appearing in a new place, fabricate reality not with lies but with concrete and steel and large support structures and good manufacturing, if I can I will and I have a new suspicion that I actually can, just because you don't think it's possible doesn't mean I can't spend my nights and weekends practicing bending metal spoons with my mind, if you're going to give something up let it be a bad habit or a bad influence not your goals, I've been talking about relentless positivity for about a decade now, quitting usually teaches you the lesson that you shouldn't quit, perfectly soft fur, one of the most difficult types of struggle is when you start to believe you are not even worth anyone's effort especially yours, he was a fire breathing dragon of a human, any which way that you would like, the colors were more vibrant there, an attitude like anti gravity meaning entirely theoretical, formidable faith in the relentless passage of time, learn what you can actually count on, an absolute unending vista, burrowing deep down into the Earth, politicians campaigning with their fingers crossed, who gets to decide what is and isn't allowed, some of us have never learned that it takes all kinds, have you ever felt your passion in your belly and your lungs and on fire in your brain, a place where even the plants are dangerous and mean, my life's work is extremely susceptible to a house fire, put it in a drawer and come back to it in about seventy five years, learn all the synonyms for the word gratitude, I smelled fresh biological nitrogen and oxygen for the first time in months, especially don't give up just because you don't understand, exercise your prefrontal cortex daily or you might lose it, dictate your truth and your needs, I'm sorry if it's a stupid question but wouldn't a quantum leap be really tiny, I bent my white matter just thinking about that one, frogs just kind of look funny, it will always be funny to yell a random phrase at a pedestrian as you drive by in your car, completely innocent mischief, I hope the script to my life is a comedy but it seems like I might just be an extra in somebody else's script, I probably won't shake this feeling of inadequacy whether I reach some form of conventional success or not, keep what really matters close, who said have a cow first and what did they mean, the possibility that the payoff is not as good as the anticipation is the number one reason you should just enjoy the act of creation, a work of art that completely absorbs my entire attention span, I cannot rush it because I'm locked into the pace of the ticking second hand, I want to let it all happen but I'm thinking lately that I would probably also cut my thumb off for it if I had to, trying to tell a kitten that I'd rather you didn't, I've never told a story that was painstakingly accurate, it can all break apart far easier than any of us really like, writing is mostly just counting the blank pages unless you write on a laptop in which case it is mostly just looking around for your charger, I wouldn't be that surprised if I have the opportunity to float in space before I die, the slow roasting of society, every tool that we have ever used has started in a human's head as just a silly idea, building yourself into an intricately layered person, just fix it up until it was better than before, using dramatic effect in a boring weekly corporate office job meeting, how many adjectives can I fit into one sentence, pile up what little good you have and appreciate the fuck out of it, I'm only this positive because I got really sick of being around negative people, a grandparent of a grandparent, they think their criticism is pointing out a fatal flaw when really they are almost always making a huge deal out of a minor detail, don't worry about making a name for yourself just grow an iron stomach and take good care of your spine, the stupidity is stupendous, medium rare, I went from a full sprint to a dead stop, I will be a very different person by the end of writing all of this, I wonder which aspects of my life are fictional, I think I will be okay with the realization that I am really not ready, I don't know if I've ever been aghast, what is an experience that no one has had before or will ever have again, I am now part of the crap that is out there, you will never be able to say that I didn't care, build a statue in your mind of any person you please that is as tall as the tallest building on Earth and then have the statue come alive and swim off into the ocean, they broke it open only to find it was full of sawdust the whole time, up to you, can nature remain in balance without its violent predators, who I meet will shape what I make, my mistakes have thus far yet to cost me my life, just because you are taking something seriously doesn't mean others will take you seriously, we currently cannot levitate because our powers are severely needed elsewhere, vague sources, bring a notebook, there is coffee on the counter, alright already, I trust the wall of text on the internet at this point, insanity on a comical scale, soon computers will do everything and we won't know how to do anything, if we had just an hour or two of extra daylight the entire world would calm down, genuine garbage, we all have a mental garden growing wildly different crops, we look out in front of us and shape what appears, our meat suits expire like any other deli meat, parachute into your favorite sports stadium, I just want my soul to be able to say that I did what I came here to do, when you find yourself second guessing just prove yourself wrong, build up those around you and the people around them too, a message for anyone stopping by, I think part of me wants to just live the mole person lifestyle deep under a city in a vast tunnel network, stop saying bad stuff about others and completely meaning every word but if you're joking you get a pass, the many accidents which we just accepted as the truth, the history that we are being forced to uncomfortably live through, insistent on having fun when it seems like no one else is, the fewer the future atrocities the better off the entire planet, if nothing else ever works out for me I can always fall back on my knowledge of science fiction fantasy hero and villain power level ranking charts, the emotional damage caused by biting down on the fork when you're eating, organized and curated psychedelic dream scape library, run straight into the unknown like it finally doesn't matter what you're running into, diamonds shining in the sky after snow falls off a tree branch, I'm sure there is a way to have a human society without destroying everything else, my brain can't take anymore bullets, the consistency of change, I can feel the walls breathing, it will be a great deal different in a very short time, some people are totally unaware of the causes of their feelings, we are dealing with the same level of evil as a thousand foot tall monster attacking the city but the world doesn't work like old science fiction so we cannot all see the monster, my master plan is to get myself to think in ways that I haven't thought yet, as good a place to rest as any, some are born with a list of violent enemies, the doctor told me I would feel a little pressure but it was definitely just regular pain, you need to transfer yourself from a planter to a field to ensure proper future growth, the vegetable intelligence network, riddled with misspellings, you will find the unexpected along your route, eating healthy and finally feeling the difference, we made thinking machines as similar to humans as we could and it turns out the main thing they are good at is learning, make sure the artificial general intelligence fully incorporates all the greatest spiritual teachings that we have, there is a constant power struggle between both of my cats for a hammock that is both comfortable and provides a perfect vantage point observing the entire living room, just focus on love, you can numb your emotions if you want but you can numb a broken leg all you want it doesn't mean you can walk, what level of good am I actually capable of achieving, discovery of higher and higher truths, none of that matters here, part of me is terrified so I'm working from the other part of me, I met this guy that had a well-trained hamster in his sweatshirt pocket literally everywhere he went, there are facets of yourself that you are yet to fully understand, I've been trying to tap this untapped potential that I keep hearing about, I thought your dark night of the soul was supposed to come and go but mine seems to come back a few times a year, the ways are many but your path will be one, acknowledge unique and differing perspectives, we should be growing way more food, I've heard the warnings and I have chosen to continue, the most sensible path is oftentimes not the one you should actually take, wet blanket theory, I really forgot what I meant when I said that, what can I help others with, think of how difficult some back breaking manual labor jobs are and then spend that exact amount of effort on your passion, it would be fascinating to have an interdimensional being explain the secrets and meanings behind my genetic make up, there are so many people telling you to follow your heart in so many different ways but you're still not, which of my sixteen great great grandparents do I most closely resemble, at this point I have enough reason to believe that my life will continue on the path of love, I'm currently processing, a healthy dose of pride in one's self should ward off any unnecessary self pity, you'll only ever go further by going, face forward into the flow of time do not turn your back against it, being stuck paycheck to paycheck is one of the greatest traps that the swindlers have ever set up, I feel ashamed, we are alone in our most important choices, beware on your path following the breadcrumbs, you could jolt awake at any second and be a different being waking up from a nap, someday you might ask the question of what is and isn't real and you won't get the straight answer you always counted on, what exactly is happening when we imagine an event that has never actually happened, there is so much we don't know, the you without your character and your spine is no longer you, accidentally drinking heavily for a number of years, the sum of every one of your actions has led you to this little line of text, we will be dealing with worse problems in our future, if you are misled and told a small nothing of an action is a misdeed you might lead yourself to larger wrongs because you've thought you always did wrong, we may never know true justice, I'm certain I can do better for myself, we have a common enemy there, I'm glad my asshole of a friend asked me if I was really doing my best in a condescending tone, lift the curse of your entire family's lineage, there is a lot more going on behind the scenes of this reality than on this little stage we all share, your life will have its crescendo, the aggregate of all the laughs you've ever shared divided by the sum total of all your tears, it makes more sense this way, pre-load your deja-vu by imagining detailed aspects of all your possible futures and then try to bring them to be, who are all the passengers on this strange ship, you'll have to slowly build up to your wildest fantasy, put yourself through ordeals of your choosing, I do not plan on reincarnating on this world ever again, why all the cages, you will find out when you push yourself, I would rather walk across a busy highway, stop doing all the stuff you don't want to be doing, this isn't it, I was expecting to come across more riddles and puzzle solving as I grew up, I would pluck a nose hair every thirty two seconds and deal with that annoying pain the rest of my life if it meant I could have my chance, she made earrings out of flowers, stare up at one particular star every night to make sure we're in alignment, admiring an ancient megastructure, look down at your feet, fear for your safety, it might never be what you think it's going to be, we've all secretly enjoyed catching a cold because it got us out of certain obligations, as smart as the computer was the human's first order of business was cracking its code, for me, is it possible letters and digits compose all of man's thoughts, not only is our moment past but soon it'll be ancient history, my current goal is to be undeniable, consider everything you do a time capsule to look back on fifty years from now, we are all very busy thinking, guided meditations for the complete and utterly mad, I would prefer mixing all our thoughts together in a big soup, maintain forward pressure, it sounded good, who are you to say what I can and can't care about, snippets and imagined conversations, watch out, I'd tell the secrets of the universe if I knew them, if the theme keeps repeating it must be important to me, eventually we'll have to do better, my insecurities melted away one day, eventually they are going to try to make you hate someone you're not going to want to hate, never call it insane just because you don't understand it, laser focus, uncover what you can, what is on your quest log, we bought our small slice of paradise, a country of rebels, can we all take one or two steps back from the edge, they want us all to think the worst is coming so we stop striving for the best, a fresh hot meal, what will you do with your incredible small slice of time alive on this Earth, I can barely count, to trick myself into thinking I don't need an incredible outcome, a situation no one could have ever predicted literally every single month of every single year, bring what you can and let's run, rest easy, tell my mother that I love her, don't be afraid of spice, if you watched my life like it was a movie and you were the director I want to know what you would change, the strange learning curve to listening to what your own soul is telling you, the elites seem to have no intention of fixing anything because for them it is already fixed, grow your future self, placeholder for ten million words, after market shoelaces, don't pick at your wounds, the transition from a low level practice to a high level execution, making the rare attainable, there are few who would fully agree with me, feeling out ahead of yourself in pitch black darkness, we might have even less of a chance than we originally thought, don't miss your opportunity, your gibberish is another's truth, cruising altitude, our leaders are constantly lying, clean your limbic system out, I won't be surprised during my reckoning, hours and hours invested in each other, I can't really wrap my head around a single trillion dollars, watching documentaries that are way over my head, call it what you shall, we're not ready and its coming, where should we go next, I just want to hit a trifecta, people are disappearing, can you wad up my life into a ball and throw it as far as you can, there are long unexplained mysterious sounds coming out of the ocean and we just shrug and keep chuckin' ordinance down there, I hope I see Big Ben or the Eiffel Tower one day, we are the road as it takes its turns, so much more is coming, I might be able to understand eventually, imagine how good it's all going to get, my plan is to not tell anyone my plan

†

MY PLAN
IS TO
NOT TELL
ANYONE
MY PLAN

Positive/Negative

+

The beings are with us now, our brains are so negligible when compared with the big old sun, we forget every single time we are called the best, congratulations are temporary, your potential energy is boundless, to think of all that has happened in just the space of an inhale and an exhale, it is vitally important that you do not sell yourself short, I want a chance to really do what I am capable of, to get out of a bad situation you first have to recognize it as one, we are operating under the assumption that all of this is explainable, when you accept the nature of change your outcomes improve, the stand offish german shepherd finally got lonely and curled up at my feet, if I were a fish I wonder if I would eventually figure out I was in a tank, displeased with the overall way we do things, I find it exciting to think about the questions that we don't have answers to, we're getting better, I now know what the teacher meant when he instructed us to surrender, it is okay to not be feeling your best because your best is probably yet to come, there is no telling where the payoff will come from, an ever asking question, sleep with memorable dreams, investigating the intentions of a ladybug, the folly of our own perceived intelligence, what are you thinking when you're not consciously thinking, not only is it coming but it's close, what would you do differently, all these miracles and we still demand magic right before our eyes, appreciation for the mundane and often overlooked, if emotional pain acts similarly to physical pain and we still hurt from an event that happened a long time ago then reason says the wound never healed and scar tissue never formed to protect it, we are able to heal because we are also continuously growing, all the answers are available right here in our universe because all the questions are emanating from right here in our universe, cast your critical eye elsewhere if it isn't truly helping you see, today I rambled but tomorrow I'll make perfect sense, they outlawed the triple edged sword but the drone strikes are fine, your hero has died, there are no words suitable for such a tragedy, not only will the world keep spinning but the plants and animals will keep breathing and living, add a little extra of your own salt and pepper blend, like the fact that you will continue discovering aspects of yourself that you had no idea were there, if the machine is headed off the cliff then be a spot of rust in the gears, when you truly and finally fully commit you will discover hidden parts of yourself you never knew you had just to strip them away and feed them to the cause, I could hear the drums of war in my sleep last night, not only is this chapter over but we are on our way to the sequel, a vacation for your psyche, promises kept, I'm proud of myself, how we each individually choose to deal with the horrors is up to us, I could feel my life quickly turning during that time, discovering your purpose then provides the world with that purpose, I'm building my own ethos as you read this, we all hear the teachings eventually but not everyone listens, I need to eat healthier, I didn't expect this and that seems to be the whole point, demonstration of art, allow yourself to blow away with the next breeze, beware those who believe it is all coincidental chaos, there is deep power in calm, commit to a project that is far bigger than yourself, when the tree dies it goes on to build our structures, just breathe slowly in and our of your nose, my stomach hurts, the seconds will start to matter a lot more than we used to think, my advice is to truly listen to the advice being given to you, your purpose should ring like a bell within you, focused mind wandering, my youngest cat never really understands that she is in trouble, the more people you pray for the more the world prays for you, if the destination were already decided would you even want to know the location, every small act we make has an impact on the largest aspects of our life, the more adventurous the aspiration the more exciting its coinciding journey, the truth is intrinsic and instinctive, I got all that I was supposed to do today done with a little extra time too, do not lose your playful nature, our most valuable lessons are so true that they even make sense when we place them in fantastical fictional worlds, I've lost interest in all that used to interest me because all of my attention got vacuumed up by a brand new interest, throw convention off the highest bridge in your area and begin what hasn't been done in decades, a subtle type of sweet that doesn't stick to your teeth, we stopped recording our dreams a long time ago, rise to your own occasion, she accepted me, we all have different start and end dates, can we just do this another time, there is a constant presence of another human's opinions in my head and I'm now officially tired of them, I'm done being sorry, we need reliable realities to be the anchor point for the less reliable ones, the power in an individual to bring their imagination to reality, the strength acquired through dealing with countless obstacles is within you, a forgotten memory in the back of your closet only brought out during a deep spring cleaning, you have something to show for all that effort now, I've had a great deal of trouble accepting my emotions in the past, the feeling you get when you arrive, faster than your legs alone can take you, learn to tune out the buzz so you can really listen to the hum, focus on finishing just one of what you've started, grateful for each of my mornings, brilliant in a bright as the sun type of way, we're all just trying to survive, you'll really feel it when your dream makes the switch from fantasy into a concrete goal, the game where your opponent sees your cards, stir yourself awake from your ignorance by studying beyond your current understanding, the more weary the travellers the more relief in the destination, I hope what is looking for you finds you, mirror calm ocean in the morning, don't squander your life, strive to widen your views, go make an absolute fool of yourself and call it life experience, enjoy the rise, dedication can be difficult, your best option is likely not your easiest, going by the feel on your fingertips and what makes your hair stand on end, knowing nothing provides the liberating groundwork for discovering something, don't pretend you don't have any demons because then you probably are your demons, ask more of yourself then what others ask of you, I will have to clarify much of my own thinking with future writing, can we help, jail break the code that is running your simulation, don't lose that thought, the promotion of a pawn, that's a very thick book, for once I am happy with my choices rather than tearing out my own hair in regret, an honest motivational message is that recovery is not easy for anyone but possible for everyone, if I were to spend every fraction of every second obsessed with my work I wonder what would come out of it, they found the code running the universe on an old server in a public library basement, some people have no interest in learning to think differently, I want the best for the next five or six generations of humans, there is an alien intelligence living underwater underneath the Bermuda triangle, your only chance at succeeding is in trying, I hope the quotes in this book are not the only things encouraging you, every second is your turning point, the world will chew you up unless you are hard enough to break its teeth, young enough to want massive change and old enough to be ready to execute it, listen to what your intestines and your abdomen are telling you, the lofty goal of reaching millions of people, take the risk of being misunderstood if it means you are finally expressing your emotions, it is nearly impossible to pay attention to the monumentally boring, we will do all we can for our sick pet, you might be held to a standard that doesn't even correlate to your own scales, don't let anyone tell you you're a bad person, I choked on my own breath just thinking about it, of all the predictions we made when we were kids which ones do you still want to be true, be careful with trying to die because you really might, you can get blind sided by your lessons or you can go seek them either way you're going to learn, find what you would enjoy failing at, I'm giving myself Super Bowl half time locker room speeches in my head at four thirty in the afternoon on normal Wednesday, the controlled madness of imagining a society on a different planet, take your life off cruise control and floor it for once, a metaphor that just makes perfect sense, what shape are you carving out for your future, use your pain to build if you have to, I spent the afternoon praying, purpose in every second of every action, the notion of proving oneself now makes me sad because we should never really have to prove anything to anyone, you may have no idea where you are taking yourself but you're going, the power of consistent minor changes compounded over time, spend a whole afternoon just feeling your inhale and your exhale, you were an asteroid once and you collided with the moon, no one alive knows what we will all know when we die, pursue your passion with love, build a jet car in secret in your garage and fly two hundred and sixty miles per hour down the highway never to be seen again, you're enough, uplift a few just a level or two on your way up they will thank you for it, try not to be upset with your sequence of events, the noble quest of attempting to understand who we are, if you're upset with your progress just think of how strong a foundation you would like to have, tomorrow will be great, you could fall asleep tonight and never be you again, we were all too tired for the call to action, there seems to be a major uptick in guys climbing skyscrapers without ropes in the twenty first century, you can drift or you can swim both will keep your head above water but only one will move you where you want to be going, I have a message for you but you'll need the secret code to be able to translate it, it's a weird balance between going easy on yourself while also going as hard as you can possibly imagine, collapse the wave function of your life, learn to listen, it is life changing to finally realize your dissatisfaction is a very good thing and that it has been driving you forward all along, confused for months only to randomly fully make sense in a second, they really appreciated that invite, some people never even start their magnum opus, I'm happy to be one of those monkeys at a typewriter with no clue what they are doing, you can get a clearer picture of the future if you focus, think of a creative way to spend your next free day, have we always been like this, a concentrated effort of force toward what you really want, it seems that before beginning a human life every soul agrees to experience unbearable and excruciating mental and physical pain, even if it were up to me unfortunately

I have very little idea of how to make this world actually better, talking about politics always reminds me of those guys that call into AM sports talk radio and explain how they could have coached the Patriots better, some cuts heal and you forget them but othertimes you lose a limb, when played back there really are three acts to our lives, once I worried about my fire going out but then I learned it was a nuclear fusion reaction, no promises yeilds higher success, I would go back to the drawing board but it is in a different time zone, you are an antelope thrashing still alive in a lions jaws, I listened to the motivational gurus and now I'm here, appreciate depth when you come across it, you've been fighting since you were ten now it's finally time to rest, that feeling of coming to a realization, take a waterproof notebook out in a canoe in the rain, that level of surfing where you are excited that a storm is coming, sorry I wasn't listening I was just thinking about a group of sasquatch playing baseball, my thoughts got all tangled last night, part of me just wants to sell snowcones on the beach and sleep the rest of my life, fluctuating between a drive to be different and the instinct for the ordinary, blowing your mind to pass the time, reading about things you probably shouldn't be reading about, spend five years making an indy cartoon for you and your friends, I suspect there is a picture that is too large for my neck to strain to see with colors that my eyes cannot perceive, would you do this one over or do a brand new one, you're a factory of thought so what are you producing, how many action potentials firing through my neurons does it take to make my inner world, I would like to go against all the odds please, how can we foster the feeling of doing better in as many human beings as possible, to tackle life's greatest mysteries during all your off time, I like the stories about internet sleuths successfully solving major crimes, thousands of years ago another person sat at a similar table and wrote their thoughts down on papyrus, your past life ended on the front line, the strength and consistency of a waterfall, be the proof you need, I would like to find out which thoughts others use to get them through their hard times, the beat and rhythm of our lifes plays a unique music, I a have painful feeling that I can do no right, to do despite not wanting to, what flavor is your inner monologue, wisdom should never be kept secret, what are you personally doing with the access to unlimited knowledge that is in your pocket, I feel like the universe is large enough for Star Wars to be taking place in a real galaxy, if you are reading this thank you, your future might not be ready to be your present yet, seek an ontological shock, changing your mind effectively is a skill worth learning, I'm grateful for the people in my life, welcome the change that you have been asking for when it finally knocks at your door, understanding of your own ability, do not underestimate the genetic memories that are locked within your bones and blood, we are made of basic mud and clay but the electricity that is keeping us alive makes us divine, what can I even want that is truly worth having, it looks like I write something about a dream on every page and I'm not sure what that says about me, can you hear what the mountain is trying to tell you, I believe the state of the unknowable or the yet undecided is a crucial element to the fabric of the universe, you'll stumble on your place one day, I've thought a lot of wrong stuff, all we have is a few milliseconds of the present moment and the rest is faulty memory, nevermind a second chance I'm on my fourth or fifth, I wonder if I will ever swim alongside a blue whale, I would be very happy to find that the afterlife is an endless library of worlds and souls, I'm sure this is crap but I'm enjoying writing it, I fell asleep on a cumulonimbus, some people always listen to their self doubt and you should try not to run that risk, imagine if God actually came and told you you're off the hook, I got shadowbanned for posting poetry, to create something that was not there just a few moments before, to change the definition of an ancient word, weird argument, many of us have forgotten how to light fires but we know how to wield artificial intelligence, to be proud of a part of yourself that only you can recognize, a rambling conversation over hot food, a catastrophe and a masterpiece are cousins of words, you seem to have a different outlook than you used to, soft green moss, the spicy smell of electricity, to hold a room, never brainwash someone, act accordingly, the smartest is the one still trying to learn, the world could end any second but it doesn't, I'm not sure, performing even though you're terrified, never buy from the salesmen that is trying to scare you, crazy how we are able to use two dimensional symbols to create multidimensional feelings, the results of your life's work were a miracle, how many scientists invented free energy and got killed for it, risk sounding corny or never sound genuine, you can do anything you want with your temporary license of consciousness but remember that it is temporary, what can you do for someone that you really wish someone would do for you, let's get pancakes in the morning, do something now so you have something to look back on later, ultimately I just hope a few who are suffering find some relief, do not avoid what scares you, you might be running out of time but so are the rest of us, remember the guy who solved the Price is Right, I'm not crazy, the cross road between reason and insanity, try to hold two conflicting thoughts in your head long enough to possibly think of a resolution, don't worry about your shortcomings you make up for them plenty, try to make a sad person happy this week, who was it that said the moon rang like a bell, we're not on a rollercoaster because there are no tracks, always see for yourself, I don't think they're going to be able to build the machine that they are trying to build, mean no harm but do whatever, self discovery is endless because we're someone new every year, you won't know until you look back, one of the rules is that you can only find what you are looking for when you are least expecting it, you will have your time and place to weep, the secretive feeling that all is going according to plan, what is the most important question to be asking, you'll have to lose sleep obsessing over your goals for a little while, fresh ink, a broken finger and a busted tail light, I'll have you know, I want a QR code tattoo, there better be more to the story, all I would like at the end of this life is a few good answers and many more questions, there is more for you in this world than you could ever possibly know, there is your invention, when was the last time you spent a full afternoon thinking about just one thing, it won't all unravel unless we start pulling at these strings, worldwide clean drinking water, our cosmic shift occurred a while ago, be good, I feel like dogshit on the bottom of someone else's shoe, we're lucky to be seeing just a sliver of all creation, you have the uncanny ability to bring about what was not there just yesterday, the eternal hobby of carving very hard stones, I know I'll never be perfect so I am going for quantity over quality, think with all your might, you never know what will be your ticket into the eternal party, the satisfaction of a truly good deed, if I write good enough this might be read in a few centuries, a generation raised on incredible dreams and surviving incredible disappointments, not all of us ever get the chance to be proud of ourselves, it is a shame how much is forgotten but maybe remembering is not the point, what is real for me is not real for you and vice versa but hopefully we have at least a little bit of overlap, a dreamscape made of letters and words, you may have to lose your mind to rediscover your soul, take all the time you need, there are sculptures that are thousands and thousands of years old, many have tried to justify their evil while good has never had to be justified ever, freedom within the limits of physics, you shouldn't have to punish yourself to succeed so if you keep lashing your spine it might be time to stop, what has combined to form me, remember your billions of neurons and give them some good information to fire over, change your mind frequently and often to improve your thoughts, it should really only be liberating to learn you've been wrong, I wonder what creature is looking up at our sun as just a tiny star in their sky, the strange impenetrable love for all things, spiritual mistakes,

I'm only asking you to grow because I'm sure you can, don't commit suicide until you've really given yourself a chance to live, not everyone understands but someone does, we've suffered a crushing defeat but we still have to continue, you would have been best friends if it were not for arbitrary circumstances, accept the wisdom that is floating in the air around you, the number of miles that our feet can take us, I'll crush my hopes between my fingertip and rub them into my scalp and thighs, we might not get a chance to understand in the future so try as hard as you can to understand right now, I hope you start to hear all the things you've been trying to tell yourself, thank you for noticing, that small interaction made the day better, what would happen if the alphabet had twice as many letters, there are infinite ways to express the same truth, you will deeply feel your purpose when you are lucky enough to grasp it, if you were going to die next Friday where would you be from Monday to Thursday, I'll admit here that I've sat and cried tears that I had trouble determining as either happy or sad, open your heart to the possibilites that you want the world to show you, your pain is helping you, do you see the glow over it all, what'll you do next, what are you completely convinced of that others almost certainly wouldn't believe, we can fly into space we just don't, I'll keep my hopes but only if you share some of yours, you'll find your wonderful state of being one random day, my favorite teaching is that none of the spiritual teachings are riddles that need to be deciphered, the purest you that you could you, I've found truth through mistakes and accidents more consistently than the truth I sought so hard to find, some people enjoyed it, I really don't know what to do with all this sorrow anymore, you'll be surprised what you can do once you start patting yourself on the back rather than kicking yourself as hard as you can, your perspective is sharp with a clarity that no one else can see but they see equally clearly through their very own, my intention through this work was to become a better writer but I might be lucky enough to become a slightly better thinker, I wonder what the teacher would have said if I tried to write this for school, be overwhelmed and then recover, I'm grateful for the way I think because I feel like I've had little say in the matter, alienation is pointless, try to be grateful for your shoes when you reach the top of a mountain, I'll take no credit for my accomplishments and full responsibility for my wrong doings, babe you wouldn't believe it, I would love to be more mindful but I actually just started to enjoy my racing thoughts, be happy with the effort you put in, I've broken many promises which is why I want to keep them so bad now, take me for a ride, I understand that it can all only happen when it is ready but God do I want it now, I hope you have a good day today, some transitions will be effortless but others will hit you like a bus, I know you're doing an excellent job today and I'm not even really sure what you're doing, I went to purchase a few fucks to give you but the fuck store was fresh out, just a few words here and there for a couple years, rock your own world or it will be rocked for you, the boot is on our neck but we're going to buck them off, I think I would have more fun being thought of as crazy than ever being taken seriously or god forbid ever considered smart in any way, we arrived a while ago but our legs just won't stop walking, a self driving soul, we don't mind the small bites from a kitten because they're just tryin' to learn what biting is, we have this hunger and thirst for greatness but we barely acknowledge the greatness we are already a part of, for the love of God please burst my bubble, if anyone is going to space then I can follow my dream too, the first thing to stop a person from achieving their goals is their own belief that the goal is too difficult or unlikely so they stop, we took the canoe out before the sun came up, the book I was waiting for finally came in the mail, you never know what will change your life, orient your trajectory to rise instead of burrowing further down, brand new shoes and a brand new hat, I'm convinced I'll find what I'm looking for, a dive bombing corkscrew maneuver in a commercial airliner, spiritual allergies, categorization of humans is inherently wrong, the human body and brain heals when it is taken care of, if I run out of paper I will have to write words all over my legs and arms, I couldn't believe what my eyes were seeing but my heart was there to bear witness too, is there only one present moment across the whole universe or are there multiple, would it feel good to know you are halfway or would that feel like not far enough, the universe is code on a paper napkin that got folded up and forgotten, pleasing to the thoughts, they escaped on rollerblades, I don't like the thought of an alien pausing time and making minor adjustments to my life without my awareness, an icy treat on a hot day, I'm going to hit the road, following your heart is of dire importance, if you are a kid reading this skip school, unimaginably strange, many of our thoughts arise from our gut, our story isn't over if we're still breathing, I'm excited at the prospect of brand new ideas, a more stable dream, we're all in the process of doing the best we can, rephrase your own thinking, you'll have new light tomorrow depending on the weather, I can taste blood in my mouth but I'm not stopping, stand up for your perspective, there is an art to making a complex concept understandable, I'll always remember my first best friend, a minor adjustment which set your course through history, what exactly would it look like for you to be living your dream, a world in which all are cared for, close your eyes and imagine a flowers full life from seeds to wilted petals, each fragment of each second that we are alive is a pure and true miracle, it is a good thing that we all must come to our own conclusions, I would love to hear your view on the nature of reality over coffee, I hope to be a bird with you in another life so we can fly together, I oftentimes enjoy dangerous levels of speed, it could go better than you are hoping for too, what if we're just in a waiting room and our lives haven't even started yet, belief in oneself is a requirement, I don't know how many humans have lived who have both stood on a mountain top and sailed a boat but I'm happy to have had that variety of life experience, all I want to do is sit and think new thoughts, I hope you can sleep in tomorrow or wake up early to do exactly what you'd like to do, I feel like I might get to experience low gravity in my lifetime for some reason, discover a new capability of yours by trying out a weird new hobby, you're trying, we're no different from the person stranded on a desert island looking for food and hoping for rain, you'll prosper as long as the sun continues hitting the Earth, for the life of me I cannot spell conscious, you and I both belong, it is curious what each of us chooses to focus on, our intelligence is telling us there has to be greater intelligence, if only we could see in infrared and ultraviolet light, what is your first memory, you fixed it, I'm a man with strong regrets, you walked all the way here from another planet, think how fast the night goes by just by closing our eyes, beware of the hatred that arises in your own heart, you'll have to find your own way, when no one comes to help the message is clear that it is time to help one's self, close your eyes and picture yourself deep under the ocean and then open your eyes and take notice of where you are, the wisdom of being a total fool, the type of engrained knowledge that only comes from making a colossal mistake, you'll cherish the time that you were alive, you are more than you could possibly imagine, if you are reading this completely by accident accept it as a purposeful message, we all carry some type of knowledge in our skulls, it will be very strange when a super intelligent computer tries to imitate us all back to life based on pictures and videos we took during this time, an electric shock to the system, you're fine, you can forgive yourself for that now, I don't want to want anything that I don't really need, have you ever seen a bird somewhere it shouldn't be flying, I'm thankful that I decided not to give up, take this all not just with a grain but a table spoon of salt, there is beauty where no human eyes will ever see, I like the idea that I am practicing rather than working, freshly baked cookies, the worst of us cannot take a joke, I'll always remember when you were there for me, deep and painful sorrow, it turns out we tend to stay alive despite our pain, I often feel a shortness of breath stemming from my self doubt but I try to practice some breathing exercises, I think gravity has something to do with importance, a small patch of grass started growing between his feet because he sat so still, part of success involves ignoring bad advice that others took, she was skilled at falling through the air, enrich the world around you, don't waste your vital energy, we are stuck here with unique quandaries and no clear answers, to spend a month on three words, don't try to rush that which has always taken time, be thankful when you are tired of bullshit, because because because, plunge into the fractal soup of non meaning, there is flow like melting ice and then there is flow like burning magma, never let them speak to you without respect, praise goodness in its entirety, I get it now, can you trust your limbic system to operate as it is supposed to, you should get a pet, if there is a static buzz that will not turn off in your head just learn to make some music with it, mess with them in good fun, technically we somehow belong to any group of people but sometimes on the very outskirts, I'm uncomfortable with the notion of living an entire lifetime and creating nothing, imagine how weird it's going to get from here, do you ever sit in your room alone and just panic about what is going to happen next, we cling to our youth but maturity is better, I said it best when I spoke clearly, never let defeated thoughts arise in the mind ever again, continue while you can, just be like your favorite animal, take your best thoughts with you, you'll have a good dream tonight but you'll forget it in the morning, there are secrets at the bottom of the lake you're floating on, flex your calves and press on the balls of your feet while you lean in to the pressure, I'm going to swim across the northern Atlantic ocean in mid winter, it's only going to get stranger and stranger and stranger, make your brother and your best friend proud, have you ever given your way a chance, I bet you there is an afterlife and only I would be able to win that bet, it was obvious to us while everyone else missed it, you'll have to wait for it so you might as well be patient, I hope I'm listening to at least some of the advice that I've been given, I wonder what catastrophe will strike next, defeat the psychopaths, I don't know why there is a trampoline on the side of the road but we're definitely stopping, collecting expensive instruments and tools just in case, you'll be happy with at least one of your major decisions, picking the perfect movie to watch, a spoonful of manuka honey, we're all literally disagreeing to agree, you really don't have a lot of time to work with before it's too late, I would disagree with a lot of this book, I apologize for my thought process, what would you change if you absolutely had to, I would be scared to time travel, we can break the rules of physics in our minds, I fluctuate wildly between wanting to rush things and knowing that I can't, we're going to lose him, there are pros and cons to being alive, you can get a lot done with a good pair of bolt cutters, part of you is inexhaustible you've just never pushed it, she took good care of her shoes, freedom in this context came with a wide open green field of grass, I never did find the right word, repeated nightmares, we were looking for some sort of revelation but I feel as ignorant as the day I started, if you are in my area feel free to call, I never want to be stuck thinking how much more to life there is, most of the message I would like to convey is that what you are hoping for yourself is actually possible, fast food mindfulness, it is going to be whatever you thought it was going to be, cold hose water, I know I've forgotten a lot of really good stuff, I'm sad, I would do this the whole day if I could, it will all come down to an arbitrary detail, there is atmospheric pressure and then there is the type of pressure that seems to come from your blood and your soul, I'm thankful for the friends that I have that people who are not my friends might consider crazy, I'm not sure if I have enough concepts kicking around in my head to do the real type of thinking that I would like to do, are you guys rippin' and roarin' yet, you might not be the creator but you are still a creator, we overlook what would put others in awe, find what inspires you and let that be what you fill your life with, it really would make total sense for us to just be a figment in the imagination of a much larger being, perfect can sometimes be a difficult word to pin down, who the hell figured out how to count the seconds, I'm so glad I learned some stuff the hard way, if you feel yourself getting scared just jump, I can feel the good happening despite the bad, it's not that we come back it's that we'll always be here, I can assure you that I did not choose my path but I've certainly chosen to continue down it as far as I possibly can, we are growing up alongside a totally alien dimension separated from us by only a thin strip of sand we call the beach, am I living each day with the purpose that it deserves, are you committed enough to completely restart if you have to, make a five year plan and stick to it, we've lived with questions for so long we're going to be shocked when we start getting answers, I just want to do what I feel like the universe wants me to, we've struck an intricate balance without even really knowing it, we are collectively misremembering events in the past at an alarming rate, look up the government cheese, I'm happy for my bullshit, there is some place you still don't know exists that you're going to call home one day, do not self destruct whatever you do, there is life if you never learn to let go and life when you finally do, a surprisingly warm welcome when rejection was expected, you won't be the same person you are today very soon, sorry I got distracted, you bought a new couch and it's perfect, that specific person that comes to mind for you, we found a cheap patch of land with fertile soil, you'll always be pulled multiple directions its called ADHD, the sky turned a color that I can't describe, are you a person with options, doing what you love even to the detriment of everything else, literary pornography, if I'm going to use my voice I don't want to waste it only being negative, it is very good to have room for improvement, you will really feel it when you're no longer aimless, a love concussion, spend a bit of time in an old growth forest, are you going to be able to say you've tried, I lit the box on fire, expert problem solver, I like being around people who aren't phased by much, we are not acknowledging all that is really there, I'm developing a healthier relationship to my self-doubt than I used to have, building intricacy slowly through patience and time, think of how much you could get done in an hour and then give yourself a month, people pleasing is a bad habit, once you do one good thing for yourself all the other ones become just a little bit more possible, taking good care of yourself is a life or death matter, all I run on is little did I know and come to find out, it wouldn't be that big of a deal to find out most of my ideas are incorrect, learn to ride the clutch, our memories are on vacation, my cat has been attacking my TV more than usual lately, landing on the White House front lawn, you're kidding, do you recognize your patterns yet, deep winter activity, we don't really need to know anymore, the chapters of our lives might be far more organized than we know, that'll be more than enough, I hope we never need to use those weird comic books that are in the back of every seat on an airplane, steal the private parking spot, am I the worst, effective curse words, I would like to live in a pyramid shaped house, I would like the help of a few good people, make sure your success also benefits humanity, what will I do while I'm still me, believe with me, I'm going to switch to writing only with a chisel and granite, return the stolen artifacts to restore balance, what if we had like nine senses instead of five, beware those who benefit from your viewpoint, we'll fall like the trees eventually, we're better off being wild, you will not know how much it will take until you arrive, how often have I been the listener with deaf ears, warm blankets, I never go to bed early, we each have our own style of passing time, audit your day to day life, I've successfully written thousands and thousands of words of nonsense, the accountability of a rickety old carnival ride, we forget that mountains flatten out over time, lift weights for a year, I will become who I am meant to be for you, I really don't want to do the same old thing forever so I guess it's time to change,

I'll have to count on becoming Lazarus if I die because I won't quit, take your myths and live them, I've found a way, colorful paint splatter against the walls of my skull, I would be happy to be one of the one's society considers wrong, I'll live in a massive derigible someday and float around the world, it is much easier to circumnavigate the globe than it used to be, it is a lot safer to have high hopes when you've become accustomed to having them dashed and are also already happy with what you have, give me one hundred days straight of effort, build an imaginary six hundred floor skyscraper with detailed notes of what takes place on each floor, we are on our way to building machines that are too big for us to understand, when will society be driven to once again build a massive stone pyramid, sleep outside, eat fresh snow as often as it falls, I can feel that there is a better way, we will survive any place we find, you're describing it as though it makes any sense, all it takes is a tiny scratch in the right place, cut a small hole in your heel and drain your soul out the bottom of you, you'll sweat through the worst of it, don't doubt what was and is being lived through, he let me hold the tiller, might have been meant specifically for you, my root chakra has been irreparably damaged by McDonalds and coffee, it takes a touch of insanity to do well on this planet, I can't be let down I shut off the gravity in my soul, tremendous effort, kill the bad bacteria with a blinding light, once you see it you cannot unsee it, feel free to plagiarize me, sometimes advice will prevent you from getting where you want to go, I can think of a reckless set of words to rattle off but I'll try to be smart with them, do what can't be ignored, bellow your truth out straight from your diaphragm, he was a brain surgeon of a trumpet player, you understood perfectly, don't be afraid of attempting to be exceptional, should could melt a diamond with a look, I had to get used to it, no one who is spiritually rich ever sold themselves short, doing as good as an American could, daydreaming and taking notes on why I see, live like a goddamn lunatic or don't live at all, he was a very harsh person but every now and then he demonstrated a soft touch, base jumping accidents are terrifying, I don't want to chase one feeling my entire life I want to look for random new feelings, my heart goes out to all the quitters because that has to hurt worse than failure, it took me some time to realize my way of thinking was a blessing not a curse, finish off your life with a personal guarantee that it was unique, I'm one of those hermetic wisdom guys, I would like to leave as much as I can up for interpretation, who knee capped your confidence and how can we fix it, you should want everyone in your immediate vicinity to be doing well, dying of laughter, we can't all go to the same exact place it would be too crowded, you'll have to be okay with writing thousands of lines for just a few good words, who made who do what, give yourself goosebumps with your own actions, love is an excellent conclusion, float downstream for as long as you have to, I'm hiding my emotions in the tip of this pen but it won't stop shaking, stop waiting for it and fucking run to it, find the place where your voice is not only heard but amplified and listened to, are we going to be the generation that starts to do better, maybe more of what isn't working will work, can you read the coded language and translate it for me, always listen close, you're as good as they come, I was someplace else, cruise control was a fine addition to the automobile but this self driving stuff is getting kind of crazy, I just want to get old and sit on my front porch waving my cane at passing traffic telling them to slow down, the natural course of events apparently includes the weirdest it could all possibly get, sometimes you are living someone else's life for them and you really can't tell until you stop, for once would you please just face your fears, some people were never even taught how to breathe properly, find some honor and keep it, it's trash but I love it anyway, be careful what you're putting in your head, don't overlook what you're good for by obsessing over the bad, carve a little space and time out for yourself, feel the fluctuations and flow with them, develop your own personal philosophy and don't worry too much about anyone else's, please include some kindness in whatever it is you're making, will I ever be all better, chase down that which keeps escaping you, I love when I have the element of surprise, growth as a goal, I'm just here to take care of my cats, that buy your mom a house ambition, my plan is to have a pallet of AA batteries and lighter fluid up for bartering after the apocalypse, I'll try to piece together my political theory through an allegory that I work out in some Star Wars fan fiction because this reality is too difficult to parse through, cool toilet paper, the feather ruffler, to occupy your entire mind on a single subject for years and years, either it's all going to work out or just some of it is, so much could be changed without any of us noticing, you're going to get crushed but you're more spongy than you might think, processing your trauma is the best hardest thing you can do for yourself, I wanted to go against all of the odds but maybe I'll just try a few first, dude think about the math it took to build the pyramids the next time you're struggling to count change, do it at least a little differently, mangled by the margins, deliver what you can, I like movies that make us hit pause and talk deeply for forty five minutes and then excitedly hit play, whichever creature is capable of zooming out and zooming out and zooming out, the worst situation is the one in which you feel you would be better off dead, learn to chuckle at your shortcomings rather than be devastated by them, what if you didn't make any friends along the way, we would probably have a much better world if it weren't for all of us, actively ignoring the bigger picture, allow yourself to see what little good might be hidden around here, if only we could feel our acceleration and see the cliff, there is neither an end nor a beginning it just goes, don't look to other people for what you should be doing for yourself, sometimes a positive message is the harshest to hear, I have a fear of being ripped apart atom by atom but I can't tell if it is irrational or not, deliberately leaving thoughts unfinished so they can be finished in multiple ways, fully charged technology, stop saying it and just live it, don't make people feel bad about themselves, there are people who have made their entire life's work the act of just sitting and being, if I have to live on Earth again I would much prefer to be just a fir tree or a fern, when you feel yourself going general try to go incredibly specific instead, the variety of human lives is astounding, you're okay, what will it be that accidentally unlocks all of my genetic memories, really we're all related or at least we will be eventually, what is all this particle accelerator funny business, what is the last thing that you did that you can confidently say you are proud of, if doing your absolute best in one location is not reflecting the best back towards you then it might be time to go do your best in a new location, what about me would you never believe, I can't tell if you're joking, I've done some of the most unhealthy things a person can do, do you have enough room in your planter bed to spread your roots, check your own diagnostics, the etymology of your most frequently used slang, you'll succeed with the same actions that previously failed when you find your correct place and time, I felt the sea grass with my fingertips and missed home, give yourself something good to think about, it is funny that carefully stacking rocks and surfing through the current of a white water river are both considered forms of balance, what will it be that totally slips my mind, I hope that I am receptive to what is eventually hard to hear, you might be in your own way but only you can determine that, rediscover magic, I'd like to break all the clocks that are keeping me on time, I'm more comfortable in my own skin lately, I would like to live near a bullet train station, we are losing a natural sense of cooperation that used to be a very natural thing, who would you like to trade lives with for a year, would you rather understand more or be understood better, oftentimes we are stuck with one or the other when it could either be a third or neither, you can purposely delay your gratification to such an extent that the moment is all you have and eventually all you'll ever need, enjoy being the weirdo and find the weirdos to hang out with, do the difficult, would you calmly and quickly see the exit, categorize this, she filled the ocean with her tears, a broken bone in nature is a death sentence, for which tasks are you most effective, it is weird bringing absolutely nothing to the table, looking for your place, coming together and falling apart, you should be able to think for a long time off just a few words, I still want my chance to do something brave, new people in your life, you couldn't tell which aspects of yourself that the others liked or if you would agree with their opinions, when you couldn't have done any worse it is kind of a good starting point, are we fixated on the smallest part of the picture, she laughed like she knew something I didn't, one day you will be doing exactly what you always wanted to do, don't go your whole life without a few good questionable decisions, morning coffee and nightly tea, we snip off pieces of our soul with scissors and send them away with messages written on them, we couldn't even break if we wanted to, if you build up enough momentum you will be moving with no effort, my cat commandeered the laundry basket, what is the funniest way to die, use your own measuring stick with your own standards to measure your own progress, learn to recognize and disengage with that which is holding you down, wake up every morning and think of all that could happen in a day, we now call our spiritual awakenings nervous breakdowns and try to treat them medically, you'll probably do better once you get away from here, nothing creates more space than time, don't be a doofus, creativity is a process, just in case I forget the code to my safe is sixty nine four twenty, you are the only one who knows what it will take, I need to start writing down my dreams again, hitch a ride on a wild thought process, if you haven't found your calling yet you need to start listening to what is shouting your name, can you tell this means the world to me, no one can show you the route up but there are so many people up there you know there is a way, no one should be testing your worthiness, do you want to find a good place to look at the moon through my telescope tonight, there is a laundry list of lessons we must learn before passing on to the next life, you're laying the ground work but you'll need to hit the stratosphere to look back down and see what you've been building, a lot of life plays in reverse, there is a speck of dirt very far away that holds all of the land together, a brittle strength or a solid fragility, the tree on the edge of the cliff is defiant, thank god it is not for everyone, be receptive, there is a message behind every stick and every blade of grass once you learn to translate what nature is saying into your native language, what would my brain be thinking if it wasn't so fixated on words, increase whatever level of understanding you are capable of increasing, I was mean and I regret it, I want to be a massive flock of birds, star bathing, make a cruise ship sized submarine, you are the definition of heaven sent, everyone gets one chance to discover buried treasure just one time in their life, I've never looked at it like that, I remember when you bought that t-shirt, fill in all the empty space with lines and color, he doesn't do well on command, chasing the transition from hobbyist to professional, there is nothing better than coming to a sweet realization, a few of the pieces have been lost, thankful for the true teachers, you'll see, I jumped off a rollercoaster and got kicked out of the state fair, whatever all this is that we are a part of it is certainly elaborate, imagine a crystalline blue landscape spreading out ahead of you but instead of a horizon the land turns upward out of view above your head, what is most important to learn is the turning point or fulcrum in which you decide what modicum of will you possess towards the ideal end you might believe is worth the risk of effort, use a thousand points to create a sphere which is then only one point in and of itself, ignore the call to action and sleep in, keeping a plague rat as a pet, do not commit suicide, the safest place you'll find is hidden somewhere deep inside your mind, crawl on your hands and knees if you have to, maybe you're the world or maybe you're just a tiny stretch of beach on a random coastline, happy as a dog getting a belly rub, your purpose has yet to be served, a smart watch with a powerful tractor beam, walk yourself a little closer to the edge to feel the breeze, encourage reckless behavior, charter a space shuttle, poach yourself like an egg in a steam room and take a dangerously long nap, flip through the dictionary occasionally, drive on the median of the highway at least once in your life, can you name even one person who has strictly played it safe and won, appreciate your lessons because not everyone gets them, I'll go my direction and you go yours but we're living on a globe so we'll never know when our paths will cross, if hollow Earth theory is true I want to fly a little cessna airplane in there one day, it really is unfathomable why we exist at all, I've seen a unicorn I swear, accept that you're afraid and continue anyway, seal up your disjointed thoughts, take your time to ramble in good company, did you or did you not, if you are reading this I promise one day you will feel alright, sometimes life feels like a log flume ride, existence can be quite unsettling if you're not used to it, an old barn in a random field, I felt it through every hair on my head, I just breathe through the uncertainty, the air was shining like a jewel thief, we've come a lot further than we think it's just this damn blindfold, some days I'm the opposite of proud of myself but other days are okay, I want to help more than is probably possible for me to help, the best advice is truly to take care of yourself, I could have been any other person but here I am being me, freshly baked sour dough bread, there is a bake sale today, donate your last dollar to a good cause, what'll we do when we're finished, I can't stop thinking about Fermi's paradox, can we please be nice to the aliens when we find them, audacious moves, be grateful for your clean water, your only opposition is you, we're gone, nothing is simple, it took a lot of water to grow this notebook, will we ever shake the feeling that we could've done better, it can be good to have someone doubting you because it gives you someone to prove wrong, big massive leap of faith guy, if you come across an escalator raising up into the clouds you simply have to take it, maybe we've been cut to pieces but our scar tissue is strong, you're a better person when you lose your negativity, this week we're watching grass grow and next week we're watching paint dry, people don't line up as many school buses as they can and jump them with motorcycles like they used to, it would be cool if I was the one to push you to take a massive risk that pays off, the clean energy that only comes from hunger, it is time, dismantle all the road blocks, dramatic results from a minor adjustment, start listening better, twenty twenty nine I'm getting heavily into bungee jumping, accidentally writing the movie script in the wrong language, her eyes passed through mine and saw more than even I knew was there, you can have the rest of me, we caught lunch right out of the river, you could change your entire future in a split second, we used to read the back of the cereal box we were so bored, become an expert in an obscure field,

I want a safety deposit box with secret agent shit hidden inside, we collectively could've done better, genuinely non-traditional decision making, you had exactly what it took but you quit, we found a perfect camp site amongst hundreds of shelves of books, you didn't have to disagree but you wanted to, no one is born fully formed it is a slow and arduous process, never postpone your passion, accept alternatives, embrace the new shape of the world when all the earthquakes hit, what would you like to ask God, there are massive secret tunnels criss crossing every major city in the entire world, govern yourself wisely but never check yourself or hold yourself back, I would've done that differently if I could go back in time and be a little less nervous, back then I didn't know what to believe so I bought into some bull shit, none of the words are going to be written unless they are supposed to be, fighting aggression with humor, we might not die in the same fashion as our ancestors, what do you want that the universe cannot provide, makes you think doesn't it, we have a few moments together that will be impossible to forget, did you ever say that thing you wanted to say, I pulled a dollar bill from underneath my fingernail, the pain of smelling good food when you're starving, there is nothing wrong with a new spin of an old tune, find the path which leads to you being better off, is all that pressure on yourself actually working, jump off the summit of the highest mountain in your area, if you'd like your branches to spread further then water your roots, the reality of the unique is nothing like that of the conformist, whisper a secret to a stranger on the subway, is your minute to minute dedicated yet, no one's dream life involves being handed everything and becoming soft, it is becoming a lot harder to be the bigger person, go wild on live TV, what did they mean when they said have a cow, squeeze in a page and a half before lunch and leaving for work, it is rude to assume what someone's been through, quickly and slowly we all grow up, not everyone gets the chance to recognize the patterns and cycles that they are stuck in so if you have some perspective on yours make sure to use it, finding and create the beauty despite the the nastiness of the world, I'm just a leaf that fell last autumn, I have this intense belief that I am a terrible person, bio-engineering gills into our necks, fulfill your obligation to live the fullest life you could possibly live, we float calmly in the vast emptiness of space dotted quite regularly with massive explosions of boiling radiation, the most that I could possibly manage, I've been a bit too selective over when and where I choose to roll my dice, we are just one speck of sand on a sliver of beach attached to a continent on a planet in a solar system and so on and so on, the blessing of a full gas tank, I have this hunch that we are all part of an intergalactic struggle between good and evil that hangs in the balance of our each and every move, my friend gave me chocolate, I cannot stop midnight snacking, male lions are stay at home dads, we know that we're wrong but we can't really tell by how much, taking a shower is like a factory reset for my mental health, how many years into the future would we have to travel to enter a society completely unrecognizable to ours with science completely beyond our comprehension, if we are an experiment then let our lives yield unprecedented results, like many of us I am stuck with an annoyingly intense desire to be unique which will hopefully lead me to create something meaningfully new but might also just alienate me and make me a weirdo, you look out across a massive field of broken spacecraft hulls and intact spacecraft with workers in space suits throwing arcs of sparks into the air as they slice off components of the ships that will never fly again to make repairs on the crafts that are heading back into the stars, although death always wins in the end we might get one or two chances to beat the odds across our lifetime, as much as I like to think I'm doing the discovery the algorithms control everything I see on the internet but that is not true when I walk into a bookstore or a library no matter how strategically they place the books, it is silly to assume we're the only life in the universe but would be completely terrifying if we are, I reject the thought that everything has been done before, have you confronted the flaws in your own viewpoint, I still don't know what calculus and trigonometry are, send me to the lunar prison colony, we can't comprehend the implications of our actions but that is how we evolved, take a dollar out of your wallet and think of all the places it has traveled before ending up in your hand and then light it on fire, I never walked through that shadowy evil valley that they always talk about, I wish wing suits and grappling hooks worked as good in real life as they do in video games, the main difference between cats and dogs is that one feels bad when they get in trouble and the other one goes on the counter in the dead of night and destroys our stuff while we're sleeping, you are melting ice worried that you are losing form but you are about to join with a massive river, I never want to be stuck in a negative mindset, stop assuming, today let's verbally acknowledge someone or something that we've been taking for granted, I don't care which philosophy brings you to being as good a person as possible to the other people that pass through your life, there is an old secret tunnel buried under your house from the prohibition era, don't get dragged into drama that doesn't belong to you, your soul has a gleam to it that you have trouble seeing but is obvious to everyone who gets close to you, my cat sees a ghost in the hallway, I hope you learn to follow your heart eventually, I wanted to kill myself but I don't anymore, there are more turns and texture in the road you are meant to walk, break a beautiful silence with a well said sentence, I'm a lucky one who heard a calling, miracles are the most effective when they occur right in front of a person who doesn't believe in stuff like miracles, you can hate all you want but the New England Patriots twenty eight to three Super

Bowl comeback was one of the greatest moments in sports history, I consume all the motivational social media content and it kind of works actually, the flowers are going to really bloom this year, the wisdom of an old growth forest, room for improvement implies freedom of movement, I hope you escape the rat race and find unlimited cheese, some risks in which you're unwilling are a no brainer to others, it used to take a village but now it takes a major metropolitan city, I was afraid to pick up frogs when I was a kid but I was proud of myself every time that I did, make an animal happy, here in the age of aquarius it is no longer an option to follow your dreams but a vital requirement, I would like to know the reason I am fighting in my mind so often, the smaller kid taking the beating always winds up tougher than the perpetrator, when you see the bigger picture will you be pleased or will it bring you to your knees, I don't know if my repetitions in this book are annoying or just the broader themes, we thought that the arbitrary was crucial and the crucial was arbitrary, what genre is your life story, the whole world is an emergent phenomena, you've done plenty you can go home now, learn how to bring it back around, I'm okay with having a long way to go, it is remarkably easy to tell me something that I don't know, ignore the sidewalk and cut across the lawn to shave forty eight seconds of your morning commute, presence is a blessing, multiple morals to each story, can you honestly say your time is valuable while you're pissing it away, once your fire goes out you'll need another spark so tend your flame wisely, there is much greatness to be achieved, the fact that you can feel more energized from exercise is hard to understand from a totally out of shape perspective, don't forget the whole ebbing aspect of your flows, I hope some of the legends are true, when the water comes you can be washed away, from planting seeds to raising crops and enjoying a bountiful harvest, it looks like we're going to go until another world war breaks out, heavy rains in May, don't idolize just respect, guidance away from where you were trying not to go but always accidentally ending up, regret and shame might be a built in emotion, place your beliefs wisely, drawn to the insane, at some point in my life I became fascinated with hallucinations, I was consistently flawlessly and ubiquitously wrong, are we still even using zeros and ones on these computers, genuinely no idea what will happen next, have you ever surprised yourself with your own reaction, have you ever destroyed something that you felt was controlling you, we found happiness where we didn't really expect to find it and sadness where there wasn't supposed to be any, are you a Webster's dictionary or an Oxford thesaurus type of guy, splattered with acrylic paint, steal home plate, you'll be called to the sage, money will not solve any spiritual issues so why is the Vatican so rich, never shy away, you lied so come clean, I'm trying to listen to all the advice of the people that I look up to but I have to admit its getting kind of hard, are we on the way to better things or did we pass them, anger can motivate but rage is hard to justify, dig a lake with your fingernails, begin a work that will take a lifetime to complete, the bulb finally went out, I'm in remission from hypochondria, sure I believe a bit too much of what I read on the internet but it's always interesting shit, just like every other day, I can see in your eyes that you have given up hope so please go find it again, the gears of humanity continue to turn, born mortal enemies, what is your favorite punctuation mark, we could have done better and we will live the rest of our lives with that fact, if your friends never encourage you then they're not your friends, my hands and feet are an illusion it's my mind that moves things, our last escapade, you've forgotten all the good deeds you accomplished, you're on your way now, grip it with all your heart, go, not everyone cares but someone will, sorry boss I got stuck in a subterranean chamber last night and I still haven't found my way out so I'm going to be a little later than expected, you will learn as long as you're alive, how much of my imagination power have I lost since I was a kid, humans adapt and overcome, beauty stuffed in all the nooks and crannies, rescue you from you, don't always go along with everyone else, the criminal operation of smuggling candy into a movie theater, I liked the concept better than the execution, salamander hunting, I would gladly kill for a basket of chicken strips in the post apocalypse hellscape, don't freak yourself out over nothing, cut down a telephone pole with a chainsaw, responsible recklessness, some risks are short lived while others take place gradually over a lifetime, you can take everything you can carry, some cliches are pretty accurate, I thought I couldn't wait but it turns out I'm going to have to, I feel like a lot of what is universally thought of as terrible is probably really not that bad, try not to be too disappointed with the answers when they are all kind of boring, I want to attach an action camera to a satellite myself to see what's really up there, the upcoming long sleep, you can't just teach a monkey how to ride a bike and then not get him his own bike, he caught the asteroid in his old baseball glove, occasionally my soul reaches out of my body and grabs ahold of something it wasn't really supposed to, hey man you don't have to tell me my artwork is garbage I already tell myself that thanks though, warm wool blankets in the dead of winter, each blank page challenges me with something to say, we run when we could walk and walk when we should run, finding profound meaning in the stupid and mundane, you will come through immeasurable excruciating pain, when we add up our lives the sum is always an imaginary number, and that's not even the best part, if we played sunrise and sunset in reverse it wouldn't look much different, a part of your current self is completely alien to your previous self, we're stuck with no guarantees but many many chances, when will you take you where you've always wanted to go, jokes on you if you try to gang stalk me I'm already clinically insane, he wrote thousands of words and managed to say absolutely nothing, augment your reality without computers, prioritize your time, you fell off all the charts, I'm uncomfortable with being categorized, when you read the papers you will find that they are trying to build a machine with a soul, if we create an advanced intelligence it will know where it came from but don't you think it will be just as interested in finding out where we came from, uncertainty is often uncomfortable but it is permanent, I don't feel any different and I think I was supposed to, embrace your options, why are there so many atoms, you'll learn, while we only get a sliver of the whole at least our little portion is dense and rich, try to view your trajectory and change your angle if you don't like your path, has it ever been safe to assume anything, what are we producing, ask the difficult questions, don't be afraid to be stupid most of us already are, look at the change from nineteen ninety one to twenty twenty four and think about the change from twenty twenty four to twenty fifty seven, I'm not patient enough, you wouldn't believe what has been seen, the moment we understand it we stop calling it magic, I like the people who make scratching at the secrets their life's work, break your unwanted conditioning, I want to go sit quietly in a busy place today, when a notebook is actually important to me I don't allow myself to tear sheets from the back of it, our bed came alive last night and swallowed us whole, we don't like to recognize how far we've come, make your own rules and then break them if you want, you'll really come to appreciate freedom once you lose it, your homework for today is to hold three conflicting thoughts in your head at once, well I guess I'm against whatever the hell that is, sensibly controversial, absolute chaos interspersed with brief moments of sanity, I've been trying to zoom out or see from the top down but I can only seem to perceive sideways, I've heard you can learn quite a bit about yourself at rock bottom so I might run myself headlong into a personal catastrophe, I feel like I need to be maced or tased just to get out of bed these days, I feel like I'm closer now to whatever it is that I'm going to wind up being, nothing quite like a well placed what, shake the branches of the tree of power and get very little fruit but cut it down and take it all and do what you want with the seeds, the walls of your mind will be laid under siege by the outside world so you better inspect the structure of the buildings in your head, we'll remember where we go, it's funny I'm so afraid of future pain when most of my past pain has healed, I'm happy I have so much to try to learn, remember to forget that later, pressure and confidence in the self combined with some level of awareness and understanding, why are we bringing all this pain around with us, I don't know if I'll ever know the why of anything, I hate watching crime dramas that go unsolved, you will be a wayward wanderer at some point in your life, seems like either nothing matters or it all does, what energy flows around us that we cannot see, our actions are not measured by the status of our lives but by the fractals of impact branching off of each and every one of our decisions, I am in the camp that believes we have free will, has there ever been a before or an after or has it always just been a now, an afternoon of acid and thoughts that my teenage brain did not know it could have, your purpose is only yours, can anyone be considered innocent after all of this, I'll put my full weight on a word or two, forgive yourself, I have a suspicion that there is some room on planet earth that houses highly secretive anti gravity technology where you can float, just crazy enough to cram it into a coherent sentence and say it out loud, we are part of a larger process that we might never be privy to, I wouldn't be surprised if we were all just characters in a book on an interdimensional shelf in fact I think it would be pretty cool, a massive string of continuous colossal fuck ups, maybe you should've, if you are unhappy can you do an audit of your life to find what you specifically need to change to be happy, it's just what I'm going to do, imagine if it works, if you could go anywhere just know you can somehow, if it only took one grain of sand to tip the scales then what can we change in our lives with just a tiny bit of pressure, something tells me we should start stacking rocks in perfectly engineered massive piles again to bring the universe back into alignment, I worked for myself and got layed off, we scoff at the ancient rituals while our own culture crumbles, will I ever speak cordially with a non human being, we are just a strange vision in a jellyfish's head in the deep sea in a deep sleep, how does one measure the inexplicable, you might not even be where you're supposed to be so just try to be where you are, befriend who needs befriending, the trick of prediction, we are never right, they let everyone think I was dead, you can cure your thoughts as easily as you can poison them, it can be okay, let your mind fall back in on itself, where did you exist on this timeline, it is not only bad but terrible, acres of green pasture with miles of fresh water river, I can't express how grateful I am to have you on my side, the song that makes you cry, remember the time you totalled your car, tuesday will be a good day this week, what was it in your life that taught you the most about who you really are, brave imperfections, vandalize reality, she had a disarming way of talking, we never should have left that clean source of water, when eventually actually happens, original ink, attitude practice, you were far away in your mind for a minute there, where will our solar system end up after all of this, not just because I can, try to recognize when you're being an idiot, the enemies of logic attacked our brain, awhile back and awhile forward, I really like gray areas, fell asleep at the flight stick, they said it wouldn't have made any difference but I have a feeling it would have, when I asked what came next he always had answer, every action we take is ancient and repeated such as eating and sleeping, you might never get the opportunity to make things right, I could withstand the harshest interrogation tactics because I hold literally zero valuable information, she held the secrets of a city skyline, unfortunately our own shortcomings tend to define us just as much as our favorite parts, whoever is in charge has some serious explaining to do, overcome your fatigue, go until you can't say you could do any better, I snuck into a boardroom meeting to see what it was all about and now somehow I'm the deciding vote, we're exhausted from swimming but it's the current that is going to decide where we wash up, experimental vowel and consonant arrangements, how far apart are these milestones supposed to be, what'll I find out next, an unidentified human torso was found perfectly preserved in a crater on the moon, are there any laws about how large a hole I can dig in my own back yard and if there are I consider it tyranny, he chased after us but luckily we were just a little faster, a feeling we won't forget, how often are our lives saved without us even knowng, how many people heard the advice and didn't heed a word of it, at this point I could find the most outlandish to be completely believable due to the effectiveness of algorithmic propaganda, you can never have enough rope, the struggle between idealism for what is better and contentment for what already is, what is it called when it all comes true, the crossed wires in my head throw sparks and are not OSHA approved, avoid technicalities at all costs, reach deeper down to find out what is there, you are crossing a terrifying rope bridge that no one else wanted to cross but really it has held for a thousand years and you are not special enough for it to fall just for you, we are made up both from haphazard broad strokes and meticulous intricate details, we found a beautiful place to breathe just above the city, what do you think your great grandfather hoped for your children's children, what do you have that you would happily die for, develop at least one secret recipe, at four thirty in the morning the water was still like glass, the shape of the temple has changed but the worship has somehow stayed the same, a large amount of the control in this world is a total illusion, I'm terrified of many years slipping by where I didn't try, speak a calm truth, pour cold milk over the words and chew them up for breakfast every morning, have you found yourself where you belong yet, rapid fire overwhelming realizations followed by a deep and peaceful calm, our generation is like have you tried being grateful and living in the present moment, you might not realize how out of touch you are until you brush up against it or it smacks you in the face, I would like to be an old-timey cartoon in my next life, the episodic rhythmic nature of the rising and setting sun, I'm not sure what you want me to do with that information, be careful lying because your honesty will slip out past the mask eventually, stone cold calm through life changing shock, dealing with the unlikely and inexplicable, now now now now now, if your life is a book who are the readers that are attracted to your story, if my hearing was as powerful as my cats I would probably also freak out at the smallest noise, either embrace the duality or search for the third, the vulnerable position you are in when you are shitting and someone opens the door, the biggest problem with the 'top' of society is their role in the subjugation of the 'bottom' of society, find and maintain a sufficient level of positivity for a good life, in my dream last night I went to sleep and had another dream, I remember a cool theory circulating in the twenty tens that said that all of reality was a hallucination caused by the levels of nitrogen and oxygen in the atmosphere, our perception of color is an evolutionary advantage but isn't it just so beautiful too, piece together your version of peace, watch your movement carefully, twenty five cent flying saucer rides, check what you're drawn to and if it's cool go get it, we got it all wrong but we had fun with our attempt, we have replaced a lot of the energy that used to be reserved for scrounging through wet clay looking for precious gemstones with scrolling through four differently priced streaming services for a mediocre AI produced nightmare of a drama to watch, you are allowed to be negative sometimes and positive other times because you are a human being, just because we can explain a lot does not mean that most things can be explained, I'm not sure which forces are most at play in keeping me sane here, I feel like the good guys are in need of a victory these days but it's been hard to tell which of these guys are the good guys, what do you think will come after all the stars burn out, we have better tools to ask deeper questions than we used to, I am pretty much certain that nothing is occurring like it is being portrayed on the internet, think of all the differences that have already been made and then go try to make your own, might not seem like it right now but you'll probably be fine, look at what the con men and the thieves make off with and think of what we could get just by being authentic, we're going to get going, I couldn't explain so I'll have to show and I'll try to explain what I can't show, if it makes absolutely no sense at first it might be some good stuff, one of evil's favorite tactics is calling you evil, say whatever you want I don't care, shield your eyes from the coming brilliance raining down from the sky, music genres of the future, party on the asteroid belt, the beings who invented the UAPs want each and every human being to travel freely through the stars of their own will but there are powerful forces who disagree entirely, we probably won't eradicate poverty before a human being walks on Mars, I'm actively trying not to be categorized but I can feel it coming, most major truths have been redacted, firmly disappointed with the constant presence of evil on this world, a silent spot on a rock just past the bend in the river where no one can see, she could say a lot with very few words, honor the thoughts in your head for you are a very rare type of being, dream of a planet and its people and then ask the sky if it exists or not, many of us who enjoy thinking so much also remember a time when being alone with our thoughts was a terrifying prospect but those times have thankfully passed, carry out a highly difficult time consuming plan, can you envision yourself from very very far away, the strange hobby of climbing very high hills, being a human is very difficult, can you imagine any other types of weather because it feels extremely lucky for us that actual water falls from our skies, you would never know how much in your life can get done with just thought and willpower unless you were lucky enough in your life for someone to teach you such things, it has become frighteningly easy for us to completely destroy ourselves, I swear I saw an eye looking at me from dead center of a thousand beams of light pointing at me, no one else should be expected to take your pain away the same way no one should be allowed to steal your happiness, there are people out there who don't want you to be doing well because they are not doing well and you should get away from them, from the heathens we were into the heathens we are, I hope you get to experience a few full circles and not too many loose ends, what are you the baloney police, we cheer on our own destruction, it probably won't matter the way we're expecting it to matter, you are just as valid of a person as anyone else who has lived and breathed, the water doesn't have to be deep to see a reflection but it has to be to safely dive in head first, I'm finally comfortable, how could I forget these times, we work well together, what do you spend all day thinking about, moving without a destination creates a much different pattern, I hope this book doesn't encompass my whole vocabulary, we're due for a simplicity revolution, it is nearly impossible to tell whether you are thinking clearly or not just look at the fighter pilots behavior when losing their oxygen masks mid flight, it is becoming more difficult to take care of yourself in our society, part of me wants to be regular but the other part of me wants to stand on the surface of an icy comet as it passes close by the Earth, you altered the course of history last Thursday but you'll never know how or why, can you appreciate the impact that random chance has had on your life and then stop calling it random chance, I dislike the compulsory, we can always change the order, what have you come across and overlooked that another would have cherished, the psychedelic experience of coming to an unfathomable conclusion, passion has always been closely related to fire so just let it engulf your entire being, I hope I find myself in some good contexts, the inherent nature of the turn of events has to be surprising otherwise the events would never turn, I would rather be committed to something than be good at something because just being good doesn't mean you'll ever buckle down and do it, we should separate the years of your youth from your adulthood like I've only been a full adult for one or two years, I want to go where vision doubles and lines blur, that isn't what you need, change the way you view your spare time, where I am now is good, heavy distortion of a clean sound, is it selfish to ask for help, don't sugar coat it's bad for your teeth, searching for every missing piece of me, what is the correlation and interchangeability of the words universe and God, I haven't known quite what I'm doing for close to thirty years now, if I didn't strike you as odd maybe we didn't talk long enough, a tool to see yourself that is not a mirror, good is the most difficult path, freedom includes dangerous options, I've been tracking the progress of a skunkworks experimental aircraft for quite a few years now, clean your ears to properly listen, who on Earth is the best representative of the human species, we won't remember more than half of what happens to us, doing what needs doing, the honorable job of the upkeep of this world, my instincts took over but unfortunately I don't have very good instincts, change the order in which the rules appear, if it wasn't universally known as morally and legally wrong would humans just be openly killing each other constantly or is there an instinctive part of us that would prevent that, I'll try not to lie, skeptical of the elites, a long long book shelf somewhere in your house, I should be doing better, this weird rock is crawling with life, check on the one you're most worried about, tranquility is only one or two thoughts away once you learn how, all this thinking and no lightbulbs turning on or bells ringing at all, a crocodile in the middle of the living room, watch out for the narcissists, intergalactic train stations, make your escape, the milestones skipped across the top of the water, hours and hours of staring at the ceiling in the shower, make enough room for yourself in your own head, finally we can breathe easy, fully embrace an artform, there has always been multiple ways to live, an unnecessarily elaborate plan, fragments of your past will show up in your future, all I wanted to do was this, brace for impact, just to say I love you one more time, go against the grain, I'm trying to leave a piece of me behind, I think I'm finally okay with the amount of pain we're expected to endure, if we were to do better what would that look like, it is very hard to withhold judgment but it is beneficial, use the dictionary, I've found myself exactly where I need to be, things change when you trust the process, I would like to either make you think or make you feel, walk with light steps looking far ahead, they keep saying don't think too much and I couldn't agree more, abandon your apathy and your indifference and allow yourself to feel, you need to wake up and live your own life, find a beautiful spot to go swimming, scare away a grizzly, I'm not sure how but we made it up there, the parts of life that are taking place outside of your body, apostrophe and contraction freedom, in twenty five days when it is bright and sunny out I will be a lot happier, I ramble when people want me to shut up, simple has always been better, your life has a beat can we dance to it, I have no idea where my life is taking me, patterns have been arising from the chaos, we live amongst constant magic, do you believe there is a powerful being looking out for you, it has always been stress at the level of omnipotence not to mess with free will, we have seen what it is like for us to not coexist, it's like we totally forget that blue sky exists just above the clouds every time it is overcast, chase the future you want or accept the future you'll get, end your ski season with a blown knee and get heavily into painting or music, what is in front of you that is jumping out at you, fresh out of everything we own, appreciate the little things to get the most out of everything, I'm one of those people too, we are way more in this together than you might think, a freshly minted thought pattern, I snoozed and losed, release the secrets, a full day in a hammock, we should be giving more money away, I'm done trying to guess where my life will go next, wash your feet and think about God, we've been torn apart but somehow we make up a consistent whole, why'm I me, I tend to write better with a cat sleeping next to me, doing everything you think you're supposed to be doing but nothing for yourself is a recipe for disaster, don't love bomb me, a complete and total asshole, curse sparingly for them to take maximum effect, we've had an unprecedented season, give me the wildest longshot of a plan that you can think of and let's do it, don't forget to use a coaster, a lot of the stuff that I choose to do is just because I'm bored, we're locked into a producer versus consumer dichotomy and the only way out is to just make something, don't go far without this book, society has always needed its rabble rousers, are you doing okay right now, what a wonder it is to find our lives are dripping with symbols and metaphors, incorporate a new way of being, I might not have the time to do all that I want to do myself but it is safe to assume that someone out there is doing some of the stuff that I wanted to do and that is great, how many people have falsely believed in themselves versus how many people would absolutely have not made it if they didn't believe in themselves, love your flaws, take offs and landings, you should always feel comfortable saying what you want to say, the true breakthrough in lucid dreaming comes when you're awake, fill your life with more of what you love, say it all now because you might miss your chance, you'll feel lighter whether you finally put down that heavy pack or you finally release the heavy thought that has been stuck in your head for the whole journey, hold your arms out and feel the force of gravity, we really have no idea of anything, are we at the stage in our relationship where we show each other our YouTube algorithms, cheese in every meal, the most potent flavors, serve while piping hot, I really don't want to argue with you, I've been trying to see the bigger picture for a while now but I think I might need new glasses, I took the backroads to get here, driving around the town you grew up in wondering what else has changed, were you a good person while you were on Earth, like you wouldn't believe, at some point you might have to be okay with being the bad guy, there will always be ifs and buts, I'll believe you if no one else does, all in one sitting, it is helpful to do a bunch of stuff you don't want to do so that you're really sure when you're finally doing what you do want to do, an overweight cat rubbed up against your leg at a party that you didn't want to be at and it made being there just a little bit easier to stay there, the moment to moment act of actually doing better, it doesn't bother me at all that my cats would immediately start eating my dead body if I died in our apartment alone because I want them to survive and it just seems like the natural order of things, you will not be the same no matter what you do, we are all brilliant as a geode when we get cracked open and polished up, make some art out of junkyard trash, move to a different climate and befriend the locals and do what they do for fun, try the strongest hot sauce on the menu, sneak in where you definitely don't belong, freaking out is honestly a fair reaction to what we have going on in this world, we are overcoming challenges every single day that we don't even notice, unpack all your baggage and get rid of what you don't actually need anymore, how do you want your life to look and can you get there with just a few minor changes or do you need to start from scratch, go to the dentist in Mexico it is much cheaper and they don't make you feel bad for drinking soda, it is funny that we struggle so hard to bring about what is inevitable, condensed wisdom, if you could change everything about you how much would you decide to keep, what would you do with your mental freedom if you had it, get it off your chest and out of your lungs

-

GET IT
OFF
YOUR
CHEST
AND OUT OF
YOUR
LUNGS

RHYTHM

♪

As you take in the vista that mountain range is in you, black ink across a white background, I have finally contributed my chicken scratch to the library shelf, no better group of degenerates to travel across space and time with, I must have all this energy for a reason, I like thinking that there is no better time in history than these past few weeks, don't let a beautiful boat trick you into thinking that sailing is not absolutely crazy, strange to think steam and ice are the same thing, society could be more creative, you're one in quadrillions, that old place will fall down now that no one is there anymore, good and bad are just poetic devices that the world uses, stop guessing where you're going and just walk, factor in some more ridiculous elements, we just watched the clouds all day, the freedom of movement in the fringe, I felt that it was all different today, we will never know why and we have to make peace with that, channel your darkness into a work of art, every night the universe has to make the hard decision of whether or not to exist in the morning and every day of my life so far it has chosen to exist, no more beliefs just certainty, I arrived last night, under the wind we do not erode we just brighten like a hot coal, my second to second experience is a combination of incredibly boring nothingness and spiritual fractals that I can't really describe, why is our reality both random and specific at the same time, even after the past ten years I still see more good than bad, we do not take part in our own destruction because we are that destruction embodied fully, how much of what I am totally convinced of is completely wrong, explain myself, we are all healing, seven gram mushroom trip, remove all the context from this writing and it proves to be schizophrenic rambling, I'm not entirely sure why everything is going to be fine, warm blankets and nothing to wake up for in the morning, exactly as envisioned, I wonder what strange stuff I will get into late in life, I think it'll be fun to be elderly and just chilling, more than what I am currently capable of grasping, smaller than life, looking forward to tomorrow's tea, I never understood motorcycle cops, doing what I came here for, open all the doors, swimming in deep thoughts, continue or die, we all agreed to erase much of this from our memories when we got here, you're not putting a computer chip anywhere near my head, the symbolic nature of four season's effect on the leaves of a tree, no one is going to think for you, surprisingly somehow getting better, I won't be the only one saying all this, every last one of them were heroes, pure happenstance, are we proud, I'm not just asking questions I actually want some answers this time, I'll be forgotten in the attic if it means that I can sleep, digging as deep as we can while we speak, not the newest gadget in a landfill again, I don't have to agree with you if I don't want to, all the tectonic plates are going to shift dramatically next year, self love is difficult to come by these days, I'm okay with all my changes, can we vote to add hours to the day, hang all the ones who follow orders along with all the quitters, a happiness charred golden brown around the edges, I connect most with those who have lost their minds, I wanted to make you happy but I was sad myself, how do you always get me to tell you things that I didn't even want to tell myself, imbue your life with the value you want it to have, they told me less was more and I still ran out, we proved the concept in approximately six seconds,

I really don't need you to understand anymore, we were all doing sketchy things and not everyone got away clean, I'm done writing with a point, I spent all day yesterday staying alive, if heaven is a real place then no soul should be deprived of one day reaching there, if you look really close you can see where the color bleeds on the edges of reality, take a long walk with this book and a pen and paper, give into your odd behaviors for a little while if they aren't harming anyone, if you say you do not believe in a God because he wouldn't bring such unspeakable evil into the world then maybe you believe in him but just disagree with his practices, why do people sometimes just instinctively want to go somewhere else so badly, not everyone will walk the same speed as us but we will find the ones that match our pace, there is no destination only milestones, an entirely new way of living ten minutes away from your last twenty years, we think it is sealed behind concrete when it's really just buried under a pile of leaves, who knows that would like to tell me, I can try to commit it to memory or I can forget everything except what I can't, give it time because it will take time either way, the twists and turns look like a scribble at this point,

I'll be the first to admit this is nonsense but I can also say that it took some level of concentration, I put a few big words in here, camel crushes in the school yard bushes, I remember when I was sad and that's why I'm so happy now, we get to decide and that freezes some but liberates others, run from the guards, your impulses will change your life so follow your best impulse, we are not using the most creative synonym we can find for basic words in our conversations anymore, there is a place in space that has never held a life-from that you are going to walk through and be the first, I would rather not try to over think what I meant, here I am reading words from two thousand years ago because there is nothing good to watch on YouTube, no one would be so mean if all of us could fly, it is interesting that two people with diametrically opposing views can each independently reach their own version of success in life, can I find a brand new way, you are going to have a turning point so let it be a good one, imagine coming up with an invention that turns out to be tried and true and stays in use for thousands of years, the little kid is wise as an old man and the old man is still a little kid, fill your brain with very specific facts about a subject that only seems to interest you, I would like to build a machine that can accurately record my dreams, sometimes I feel like my entire life started just yesterday, remember that one cartoon with the hands and the pencil, state the obvious and then say that's the whole point, what would we be without our odd behavior, when I die just give it all away, have you ever been totally lost only to turn the corner and find yourself exactly where you meant to be, we've always had at least one option, I like being around old books, the shift happened three nights ago, I never got good at haggling, I officially have all that I need, drunk on a lunchbreak and fired on a Wednesday, crushing a soda can and cracking open a fresh one, I think I'm a better person when I am thinking clearly, I've gone a decent number of years without totally fucking up now, you will regret not trying and we have all been saying that, practice your art while everyone else is asleep and one day they will ask you how you got so good at it, for the time being I'm happy that my hands and my eyes hurt from writing, it is definitely weird, forgive my ignorance, we got a flat tire but we had a spare, that was the longest I've gone without sleep since my psychotic break, if you do enough of what you love it will injure you at some point, I've never seen lightening strike so close, I don't think I want to augment my reality all that much, the skatepark of one seventy five, a freshly vacuumed carpet, I want a mentor with a long white beard that loves playing chess, it is funny how we choose to measure things, come back, sometimes the only way to truly process is to just pivot and move on, we found a warm dry stairwell to sleep in, walk across a continent, I'm easily convinced, let's go check out Saturn's rings, aggressive protection of what is just and true, do it for the species as a whole, be careful where you step from here on out, a life very similar to yours played out in the fourth century AD off the coast of the mediterranean sea, can you take these cuffs off me please, change where you sit to see a different view, seek a wider perspective at any cost, I would love a chance to work on the secret space program, it is odd that some people instinctively know what others must be taught, will all of our problems play out again with another species floating around another star, it has always been more terrifying to think that the Earth holds the only life, with continuous movement there will be moments that you gain traction and moments you lose traction but just keep the wheels spinning, my town sounds an alarm every day at noon and sometimes it wakes me up, I finally understood the term heaven sent, never back track, we are sitting on a muddy little rock spinning around an endless ball of fire, no further questions, fall out of the nest and fly, clear your blockages, I don't know what to expect so I'm going to try to not expect at all, stop assuming and start observing, I'm tired of those who criticize every little thing, how did today help further your five year plan, it has taken me a long time just for me to be able to say I'm good, get your helicopter license, you've been to the bottom of the valley and you've floated across a pond, what a unique era for us to live through, the best sex you've ever had, we're having pancakes for dinner, SHOW UP, inject all the hard truths right into your brain stem, no one will do it for you and you shouldn't want them to either, what does good support look like, as long as both my knees bend I'm going to walk and as long as my tongue wags I'm going to talk, I hate when it stays exactly the same as it was, own your weirdness, silent growth, take advice from the lakes and trees, there are alien beings made out of pure light that watch over us and protect us, we have no plans on both Friday and Saturday night, buckle up and open your eyes wide because we are going out to lunch, one fifty cc's of straight up inspiration stat, the safe route is a complete waste of time, we just barely made it to exactly where we were supposed to be, your thoughts flow like maple syrup, the cops are coming, we did all that we could and this time it worked, do you feel as capable as you really are, focus on doing a little bit better than yesterday and getting a little rest, channel an alien entity into your spare time, the truth is certainly not what they have been telling you, learning to listen and accept lessons will save your life, not all of us change for the better, morbid truth, inspect your organizing principles, multiple greats alive at the same time, each and every one of your flaws is its own triumph, your hunger and thirst are your best motivators, stop telling yourself that you can't immediately, you probably spent very little time on your most important decision so stop obsessing over trivialities, not only can we peer into new dimensions but we can create new ones whole cloth from nothing, the emptiness of space is filled with a near unlimited devastating amount of energy, quadrillions of miles travelled and quadrillions still left to go, we should place our currency on the caloric standard, I would rather have a sense of humor than literally anything else, at this point I would rather be delusional and having fun than completely sane and depressed about the state of the world we are in, a blue jay on a branch outside your window, complicated and also totally worth it, can you please just spell it out for me rather than judging me for not getting it right away, the smartest people are able to learn how to be happy, I don't sleep very good, when will the continents sink into the ocean, make new history, a kitten's tricks don't work on an old cat, the trichotomy of the human being, look how we turned out, our outcomes shall be derived through nothing but ourselves, I want to be happy for the choices that I make while I am young, we can follow a command or we can question it, how can I regret my actions if there is a life that I accidentally save and can that life be my own, how is your foundation looking, we are currently in that one time, do what you can't forget, set goals, to be confronted by the fact that you just might not be any good, I hooked my sweatshirt pocket on a door handle and it tangled me up just long enough to prevent me from stepping out into the street a moment too soon to get hit by a car, at this point I am okay leaving the rest up to totally unforeseen circumstances, have you ever in your life taken a lesson to heart, there might be some danger in sitting around all day thinking about life's mysteries, humbling yourself is a gift so appreciate your failures and losses, we all want to get lucky but how much of your life do you want to leave up to chance, as long as our blood is flowing I'm going, I really grew to like you, the unconventional almost always sets the standard, a few people with a common goal is a formidable force, if you had what I had that doesn't mean you have done what I did, an AI definitely could've written this but I like to think it wouldn't have been as cool, I don't really like thinking that we'll never know but it's true, don't misplace your sentiments, I've dropped the ball on quite a few people, luck doesn't just fall in your lap you'll have to at least stand up and walk around, if it is unlikely then you'd better earn it, not many of us will ever get a billion of anything, my plan is to just write a countless number of words over my lifetime, key to any worthy endeavor is just not stopping, our plan took us on a detour, cheese will be the currency of the future, is space too big to hold itself, how are we ever going to get this bull out of this china shop and put everything back where it was, we were totally naive and I kind of want to go back to that, I have instigated a few fights between my cats, some of my minutes have felt way longer than some of my years, I swear to God I saw a lightbulb appear and light up right above a guys head in a New York subway car, learning not to listen to bad advice, we paid off all our debts and ran off into the sunset, we fell asleep in the little nook between two trees, I lit a poem on fire today in the yard, a lot changed when I stopped making excuses, I am a powerful wizard, what strange creatures we are, you will be happy you took your time, be very careful with that door it is impossible to close once it has been opened, chances are I was far away in my own head, I want to lay under beautiful monsoon rains, I felt a little better today than yesterday, it is beautiful when you notice that you wouldn't change much of your life even if you could, I'm building my very own deep sea underwater fortress, I fully believe that the MH370 disappearing orb videos are authentic, the greenest grass that I've ever seen, immaculate timing, what will we do with all the space in the margins, I'm really not sure what comes after finding what you've spent your whole life looking for, who figured out what is edible first, I really want fruits and veggies from another planet, either stick up for yourself or get knocked aside, I never want to make anyone feel bad purposely, I found my love in a campervan sleeping in a rain storm, the feeling of freedom cannot be forgotten, I hope your bad attitude wears off eventually, post apocalyptic visions before bed with a cup of sleepytime tea, that was an odd phase we just passed through, I am too easily convinced, practice jumping for when that opportunity comes, who was brave enough to fly the very first hot air balloon, you should get a degree in being an absolute moron, not all of us will let ourselves go there, how many scandals will we have to uncover before we say enough is enough, they couldn't tell me what would happen next because they had absolutely no business predicting anything, always have at least one work in progress going, every now and then I have to throw my hands up in exasperation, encourage yourself, I really need to stop aggressively midnight snacking, we need to be consulting more with the dolphins and elephants over what to do with the planet, being weird actually gets easier and easier, if you are already floating don't waste too much energy thrashing around in the water, I hate when I try to speed up but I only manage to slow myself down, you physically cannot expect what is about to happen, the ways you've been trying won't be the way but the trying itself will come upon a new way, all I really want to do is what I'm doing right now, are you willing to go bankrupt for your dream, I can really feel that decision that I made a year ago strongly now, position your life to where you are excited about what might happen next, I never want to be caught underestimating anyone, can you honestly say you've gained momentum in the last year or do you think that you've lost steam, respect the natural timing, becoming who we were and being who we are, destroy your envy and replace it with admiration, none of this is coming with us, the meaning we perceive versus the meaning we create, today will all be gone tomorrow, spent the whole day just looking at the clock, don't forget about what is possible, there is a mountain stream with a massive elk drinking from it right now, be careful getting angry at the fact that you are lost, every day that we have a today means we survived yesterday, what exactly is my kitten thinking about as she destroys the house, what a gift that glorious change of perspective is, we have every right to exist on the planet as the trees do but the trees have every right to exist on this planet as we do, we really must be the most self conscious predator, your goals are the difference between your fantasy and reality as you stare off into space thinking about your dream, we've got a lot to give, your exertion will come to fruition, I knew a guy with bearskin pants who claimed that he had faced that very bear with just a knife, our life's convergence in its most crucial moments will send ejecta into space like two planets gloriously colliding, the big question is whether or not we have a say in what is happening to us, early departure, if you can feel yourself becoming evil please turn back now, choosing your own path is always much better than following the one someone laid out for you, embark on a perilous journey, my college professor just said wikipedia is a great resource, we have wandered long enough, levels of complexity arising from the chaos, the one means two and the two implies three which is how we get many, if you are constantly hating on everything the only thing you'll have left to hate one day is yourself, do not pollute your well of thoughts it is your only one, there is a bright and sunny day coming, how many species learned to stay as far away from us humans as possible, no better pleasure than relief from all this agony, embrace what you've been ignoring and discard what has been holding you up, a growing addiction to the free fall, we still are, lies that are so massive and blatant that questioning them makes you appear completely insane, no more treading lightly I'll just walk where I walk, learn to tune out the noise, freshly squeezed orange juice, people don't set out on perilous journeys into the unknown quite like they used to, enough has been said by the poets about the shades of turquoise and burgundy, the incredulous nature of all occurrences, there is no nil, people have been overcoming insurmountable odds for years now, I've found what I want to spend my life doing but I still have so much other shit that I have to do that keeps getting in the way, the intrinsic implications of external experiences, I thought I was a bad person for so long, resolve all the trauma that you can, at least we can be sure we're doing a little better than before, you have to confront your negativity on your own or it will consume you, instead of diving into a shallow pool take your time to find a waterfall worth jumping off, sometimes all you need is a long walk, don't complain that it is hard nothing worth doing is easy, get the contrarians to agree and you'll solve most of the problems in the world, today be grateful for yesterday because tomorrow was never guaranteed, there is wisdom in losing it all but I hope that isn't a lesson that my character needs to learn, stop playing with the ifs and start playing with the whens, there are so many who never tried calling it easy, the most difficult version of the easiest activity, what will happen when we all get past what we need to get past, the universe is busy beyond our odd struggles and occupations, I'll believe anything I read on the internet, all we're doing at this point is googling exactly what we want to hear or an algorithm is predicting what we want to hear and showing it to us before we even knew we wanted to hear it, if I could build a rocket my garage would already be on Mars, the wisdom of sitting and doing nothing alongside a sleeping dog, according to our calculations the pros outweigh the cons, we should really only ever be speaking for ourselves, I wonder how many secret agents were lost when they climbed into a weird classified Cold War contraption, what if the ants build an interdimensional vehicle deep underneath our feet, I'm pretty sure humans are going to go extinct and another intelligent species is going to come along and discover all of our crazy stuff, it is strange to think humans are probably no where near the most complex lifeform, I'm kind of rooting for the octopus for next in line for the top of the animal kingdom, trying not to kill in the most deadly setting, only engage in exponential opportunities, the wisdom of the totally insane, our consensus must be wrong, there is a battle for our belief systems when most of us just want to be left alone, everyone deserves their version of peace, we watched who we are slowly coalesce into our own final form, what can we immediately do better, for every type of pain there needs an accompanying relief, we've got more to lose than ever before and we're still probably going to lose it, I don't want to need any more than what I had this afternoon, we are in lock step together moving forward, I want to shake the sadness out of you, no more uniforms, I'm imitating that guy on the bus who has long conversations with himself, first hand accounts of what used to be strictly legend, we had seventeen harmonious seconds today, stop and feel the time pass, are you consistent with yourself, we will reflect back on our time here on this Earth, can someone please give me astral projection advice I think I keep doing it by accident, I hope no one's pipes freeze tonight, I wonder what else is out there, can you phrase that differently, are there any fully self sustaining systems, when the streetlights come on, it was amazing what we could get away with back then, starting with less than zero, hello sharks I'm seeking thirty million dollars to domesticate the octopus to be the next American household pet, did you get lost in thought today, we've only got a short distance left to go, you could tell he had the best intentions, we caught each other's eyes and never looked away, I want to tell everyone that is hurting that it is possible for it to get better, we had to take the stairs but that allowed us to talk thirty seconds longer, it'll all play out don't stress, I'm starting to like my version of ordinary, it's funny how peaceful a thunderstorm can feel, I have the utmost respect for the dumpster divers, an atomically nano-bot assembled lasagna, what do you do to keep yourself entertained without a cellphone, dedicate yourself to an unsolved math problem, we need more viable ways to make a living, I buried a pringles can packed full of hundred dollar bills but for the life of me I can't remember where, please wait for me but only if you want to, soul injury, looking out from a cave at the top of a cliff on the edge of the ocean, quadruple decker, permanently dehydrated, so far I've gained more than I've lost, do you ever feel like the reason you stubbed your toe is because you're a bad person, stop thinking about turning back, let's talk late into the night about the worst things that have ever happened to us, I've got a couple people hoping the best for me so I'm trying not to let them down, the bubbles make the water taste better, I'll have to work on an oil rig if poetry doesn't work out, it can be really hard to stop hating yourself once you start but I promise it is possible, I still have no idea how my mother managed the refrigerator so well, my best friend when I was ten helped me through some shit neither of us really understood was happening, that which you do or do not want occurring, the air conditioning is on full blast this year, did all that catholic schooling make me feel so guilty or was it just my actions, sometimes I feel a little scared of what I'm about to say, group A quit and group B kept going, produce enough for everyone, I just want to be one of those monkeys chilling in the hot springs, society is crumbling like a chocolate croissant, I wonder how long humans will stick around, I'm pleased to introduce myself for once, the beauty of continuing to do exactly what you're going to do, I got peanut butter on my favorite sweatshirt, I've never met anyone who was faint of heart, stabbing pains in my abdomen, how you choose to spend your time is what says the most about you, my bank account hurt my feelings, it's certainly a plus having someone else to live for, I feel most myself when I'm around you, I just want to do a little better than I'm doing now, video games and pizza rolls, we're us, I can't figure out how I could ever be any happier, scratch the spot on your dog's belly that he can't reach himself, does my entire generation feel like they were meant for more or is it just me, we've gone too long without talking, I really hope that there is life after death, you're a good person even if I'm the only one saying it, I planted my dreams in the garden this spring and I'll water them every day for the whole summer, anytime someone has offered me praise I thought they were just saying it and anytime someone has criticized me I thought they really meant it, fuck those counterfeit sentences, one of my favorite parts of writing is surprising myself while I'm alone in my kitchen, listen to Bukowski talk about style, I know I've done the right thing at least a couple times, you can't just say that, can anyone explain to me why suffering and art were intertwined in the first place, I don't know about a whole revolution but I would definitely be down to revolt a little, life gets a lot lighter when you unpack your baggage, I'm choosing to be positive you assholes, your hopes and dreams hurt more than anything as they slowly don't happen while your despair is the most pleasure you've ever had as it slowly recedes, record your voice and listen to it, spend your whole life avoiding pain and achieve nothing for your efforts, how do you guys tell the difference between what is and isn't real, I feel like being ahead of your time or behind the times must be extremely challenging and lonely, donuts for breakfast tomorrow, there has been a small source of warmth coming from my heart recently, check your surroundings, they carpeted a basketball court, you don't see many evangelical level atheists, you are more than one, victories come in all shapes and sizes, I think I would get along well with a beluga whale, I bet there is even more opportunity than we think there is, what is the most interesting piece of this conversation, eventually you'll go further than you think you can go, that judgmental thought was actually useless, in the process of embracing chaos, I broke each social standard to get here, my cat suckles himself because he was removed from his mother too quickly as a kitten, what are the largest active engineering projects in the world right now, what if none of this really happened, I could hear in her voice how happy she was, we should create multiple ways to feel better, we have probably spun in so many circles we've completely lost count of it all, they've been playing tricks on us since we were born, beware of the cynic, do something totally new at least once a month, what framerate do our eyeballs film at, I didn't mean to unload that on you, it looks like we have absolutely no idea what we're dealing with here, the typical lightening strike, recovering lost balance, hone in on your desires, be careful with your emptiness, people will learn to be a miser even with no value to start with, check the organizing principles, I could use a few answers so I can finally crack open a new set of questions, have you developed your own personal style for dealing with the bullshit, there's got to be a good number of differences to properly maintain the structure of the universe, it's about to go like it's about to go, what other substrates can life properly float in besides air and water, windows open please, thank God I realized I was a whack rapper, it's all fake, they built an elaborate maze but I've decided to just wait right here, I think I'll spend the rest of my day today learning about the fibonacci sequence and then tomorrow I'll go out and look for instances of it in my life, I don't know if I have the right brand of pen or pencil to ever be a good writer, love you all, it can be very fun not worrying about quality and focusing on quantity, prepare to defend yourself, pull up in a truck with your people laying in the bed incognito, cover it in powdered sugar, they always said peace be with you I hope some of it stuck, test out your zero to sixty, you should be fighting tooth and nail for what you love, failure isn't that scary when you're not starting with very much, can we please just stop the car I really need to pee, I wonder if I've ever been right on track or if I've just been wandering in circles this whole time, a cute little death machine, I hope I never have to guess, all you have to do now is keep going, we really did have a good morning, one day you will find yourself where you've always belonged, what would you be willing to do for a cup of soup, no more ideologies, I think I have some opposing views that need to be reconciled, I've yet to have the wide open road phase of my life yet, solve all your problems, are people encouraging each other to be better anymore or did we give up on that, we should move to opposite coasts and practice astral projecting for a year and try to meet in the middle of the country, you are definitely not better off for being crazy but you might be better off for going crazy and then finding your way back to sanity which can be a tough distinction to make, no one knows what is waiting around the corner because we can't see at sharp angles like that, go occasionally and carefully into that place you really don't want to go, we've become a society of habitual escapism, it's always whether or not, it appears to be a roll of the dice for many life or death decisions, how do I believe in both free will and destiny, what a great time to be a jellyfish, it's all about what you've been doing with your time in between when no one is looking, your self-worth cannot come from others look at the definition of the word, how many millennia until a baseball pitcher throws a full season of no hitters, I would like to create one of those can't look away types of works of art someday, send me in blind, let life grab you by the hand and yank you, as long as I still have my heart and soul I'll have something to spill out onto the page and the day I'm fully compromised is the day I have nothing to say, maybe this is the worst book ever written but maybe it's not either, please pause your criticism for a moment while we all take a sip of water, Koko the Gorilla always had a cat as a companion, what is the harshest lesson that you have learned so far, entertainment through fascination, the major differences might have taken place in moments we thought were small when we really didn't think much of it, I want to throw myself off a forty foot cliff into three feet of powder just once in my life, the type of pen you are using greatly affects your writing style if you don't believe me try crayon, it is much more useful to focus on your process rather than your endpoint because no one really knows where we will all be tomorrow, the whales and dolphins do have a genuine alien species to contend with and it just so happens to be us right here on the surface, you might have bigger problems than you could have possibly thought but dwelling on those isn't going to help anything either, look for effortless relationships, I've got an idea and I'm going to play it out to its conclusion, I saw a shooting star right on the edge of my vision, where can you go in your head, get stitches for the life experience, someone you know prevented a catastrophe that would have negatively altered the course of history last tuesday, genuine and calm, I wonder if I've made up my mind without really knowing it, she said take me with you and I knew that I couldn't, we need a warm dark place to sleep, I've been illegally digging a massive hole secretly on national forest land for ten years now, we accidentally broke through into human hyperspace and this is our trip, Japanese math rock to quietly sit and write poetry to, bacon egg and cheese on an everything bagel extra toasted or grilled if you can, take this moment to look back on your starting point, please take me down your strangest and deepest rabbit hole, look up the John C Lilly dolphin house, did we run out of the truth or something what is this garbage, we grew up didn't we, if your life is on cruise control it's time to take floor it for a bit, let gratitude be the underpinning of your entire outlook, spend the whole spring watching a flower bloom, I just want to be well off enough to hand out free turkeys around thanksgiving time, make sure you get your stupidest decisions out of the way while you're young, apply the way that you care to yourself, you need to be nurtured too, if you are not working on a grand plan you need to step your game up, I really want to buy an abandoned subway tunnel but I haven't found a real estate company that wants to play ball, I'm afraid of tanks rolling down main street of my little town, I'm fighting preoccupying myself, I'm just going to say one more time that we should get a half dozen donuts for breakfast, I sincerely miss my homie, we discovered what this universe wanted for us in each other, my cat desperately wants to escape, loud music, a rollercoaster in the rain, this isn't the worst loop to be stuck in, I can't think of a single aspect of life to change to make it any better, thank God for all the idiosyncrasies, you either go as far as you possibly can or one day you look back on your life and feel like you never went anywhere, grind down a twenty five stair handrail on rollerblades, cherish your connections, can you feel whatever it takes building up inside you, do you think order needs chaos more than chaos needs order, the tangents have always been worth it in my opinion, zen and the process of a free fall, I would like to get as close to flying as a human can, ahhhhhh, it's crazy to think society might need the psychopaths too, what have we grown accustomed to that we actually need to eradicate completely, we should make political lobbying illegal, we're building jumps to go even further off the cliffs now, it's funny to think our grandparents were batshit crazy in their youth too, if they aren't hurting anybody go ahead and fulfill your fantasies, your pain makes you who you are, the truth is unforgiving, that little bit we saved for later turned out to be the ration that prevented us from dying, thought provokingly beautiful, we didn't grow up because we were good enough as kids, adrenaline is the best type of junkie, the essence of a dreamlike trance, lay down in the lake and let the ice freeze over once and for good, take a walk around the planet and never go back where you started, remove the rearview mirrors from all your vehicles, pull all your teeth out and get beautiful pearly white dentures, do exactly what comes to mind when you think about how life is far too short, I want to tattoo my favorite phrases all over my body, I didn't quite like that part of me so I set out to change it, their opinion of you is irrelevant to you, come jump off the roof into the snow with us, I learned a lot about being better over this last year, I started listening to myself around twenty seven, I've been stuck in this concrete wall for six hundred years can someone please get a sledgehammer, watch the waves crash in slow motion, go where you feel like you might not belong and adapt, I haven't got solid fresh air in about three weeks, I admit to sometimes just putting in about half rather than my full best, we always talk about walking through walls but we seem to be forgetting about falling through floors, listening to conflicting views all day, stop hurting people's feelings, finish what you start after years of giving up, I don't know if we're going to make it over that hill, you'll know exactly what to do next off of instinct alone, I fixed it, cut a hole in the roof of your house to let the evil spirits out, fill yourself with the golden amber and expel the sticky black tar, your disembodied spirit floated through a massive holy chamber where the spirits reassured you that it is not your turn and sent you back to Earth, take note of what is working, he doesn't see the world the same way as we do, a large iced coffee with frozen coffee cubes so that it doesn't get watered down, either eliminate your distractions or embrace them fully, learning disjointed unrelated facts all day every day, I'm in my never ending rebellious phase, I'm sick of going back and forth all the time, I'm not going anywhere with this, I want to smuggle valuable information through an interplanetary blockade, you seem like the type that is going to rise to the occasion, give up the ordinary, we should teach the octopuses how to use computers and then we should all leave the planet and let them take over, what would you get done if you had zero distractions, you're looking out through the eyes of a wolf but you're not really seeing you're just hungrier than you realized hunger could be, I'm a little bit disappointed that it's looking like I will never lay my eyes on the great storm on Jupiter, what will be when none of us are, is anybody living vicariously through me, heaven was much closer to Earth than we originally thought, next month just live the way you've been meaning to live, if anyone would like to help me I'm very open to that now, what a phenomenal game of baseball, bring your funny ideas to fruition, flying through the trees at incredible speed playing a dangerous game with the branches, reconnect with every spirit that has come and gone from our shared little world, one day you just picked it up because you were bored and a few decades later you can call yourself an expert, you are both a sponge and a concrete foundation, I've spent very little time piecing together my own mystery, I don't know why I thought I would find a home in the fringe, some of us never get to transcend anything, maybe you have to cut one dream loose to pick up the slack on chasing another, technically every second brings something that I've never seen before, comfortable with getting uncomfortable, do that secret thing that you've been meaning to, we are allowed to hold conflicting beliefs, I wish a full refrigerator to you, do you ever think about how cool it would be to be able to jump really really high, there is no profound without the mundane, you'll never really run out of options in the way that you think that you might, we smoked the olive branch, we got stuck in our backstory, our liver and our bones make more of our decisions than we realize, there are real people waiting for us in our imaginations, the facts of the matter don't matter, lead me into a cartoon hyperspace world, we should free everyone in captivity immediately, where will you receive your meaning, break your fears apart and play with the pieces, get far away from the bad people and look for good ones on your way, we've got a million different sauces, do you think our souls knew what they were getting into before we were born, how am I supposed to know which direction to go, I can't tell whether or not society should continue, a game where even the creators do not know the possible outcomes, when they ask you to stop just politely reply that you think it's best for you to keep going, want to watch a nature documentary with me and go to sleep, the tears welled up in my eyes and there was nothing I could do to stop them, caught in the grip of the world and squeezed for every drop, how can I better cherish these seconds, where were we, would you rather fly like an eagle or swim like a dolphin, humans are nothing compared to what we once were, your grand adventure is not going to fall into your lap it is out in the world, it will be cool to see where we all end up, how smart do you think we will be in the future, say goodbye to natural shoreline, a word I learned in an old thesaurus, the moon glade pierced the clouds and gave a small amount of light, there are more types of lightening than we are willing to get close to, many words do not have a suitable replacement, pray I'm not quixotic, hope mongering, when will we strike a proper balance between delicious and nutritious, we all experienced an atmospheric shift when she entered the room, how am I supposed to find the right words when this dictionary is so damn thick, I'll give up on why for tonight, may all who wheeze finally freely breathe, the vapor of the cloud becomes the ice on the ground, she could do nothing but shine, practicality has gone out the window, how am I supposed to get better if I keep getting worse, confess nothing, I'm glad you let me know, a singularly unique type of intelligence, the toughest human life that will ever be lived, an informative talk, can we pause all warfare and just see how humanity does, I somewhat enjoyed my belligerent teenage years, every time I browse the grocery store I'm struck by what a bizarre spectacle it would be to a hungry time traveler, get really really stupidly good at just one thing in your life and mediocrely maybe passably okay at many many things, I have essentially no plan beyond one more word and one more sentence, go a hundred and thirty miles per hour down the highway on a motorcycle, do you ever see an old guy and think it must be a miracle that psycho lived this long, we will do this, the hard parts will get easier but the easy parts will inexplicably start to get much more difficult, if you have one or two people that will show up for you then you might have more than most people, unzip the sky, replace your anger with awe at the brilliance of the disc in the sky, at some point you may be asked to dig deeper and you will be shocked that yes indeed it does go much further down than you knew, punch your heart out the front through the rib cage, cut up the paragraph with scissors and rearrange it better, my kitten is having a dream about delicious fish, what I wouldn't give to be a grizzly snatching salmon from the river for just a season, you're in your ramen rice and beans phase, push your luck with gravity and eventually you'll meet the ground, I have no idea what I am training myself for at this point, you are a person just like the tree is a tree so just do what the tree is doing, and just like that it has all become what it is, the signs are so massive that we've had to become experts in ignoring them, what will happen when all the alcohol and adrenaline wear off, my leg got caught in a bear trap and I died alone in the mountains, your brush with insanity has left a permanent mark, psycho social spiritual holistic wellbeing, I'm starving but not for food, no one else owns your time, they can imprison your body but not your mind said a man who's never spent a second in a cell, I'm calling out into the void that is my self and letting the beings in there answer as they please, those little pieces of us that stay human right up until the end, we wouldn't be alive without a passion, please take me out of context and place me where you want, I don't know if I'm complicated I just don't really feel simple, what is the moral of your story, we've experienced some sensational moments in history but we're no where near done, what would my existence in the wild look like, sorry for my outbursts, when we inevitably lose it all, I hate that exasperated feeling, I might not know peaceful feelings if I didn't know their counterpart, there are very few things that will make you feel most alive in this world so when you find yours try to spend as much of the rest of your life doing those things, water the part of you that needs watering, buy GME stock, for the low price of fifteen ninety nine a month I can tell you who is really running this country and give you illegitimate legal or health advice, we finally stopped shaving off what little growth we had with our self destructive tendencies, there was very little snow on the mountains this year, how long have you been traveling backwards, are we living in a complex riddle or an obvious lesson, I just want to cross a mountain range with a bunch of dwarves for the good of the realm, I've been seeing much sharper visions since I got this new prescription, I highly advise not abusing alcohol, he was the loudest kid in class and now he just sits here quietly, the pond froze over late this season, don't seek validation in others because then they are in control of it, there are dead bodies floating in space never to be recovered, I've become eroded by the society around me and I really had no idea, humans are highly adaptable but what happens when we start adapting to destructive acts, going full circle is good but running in circles is bad, I just want to sit and think or maybe sit and not think, what were the wind chimes trying to tell us this whole time, someday you will have your last baloney sandwich, I wonder if I'll make it to a nursing home, don't forget that playing it safe is a risk too, are we an abomination, our species was quarantined in space and the ones that put us here are going to be pretty unhappy when they see our satellites and our little rocket launches, I'm a salesmen of hypotheticals and possibilities, watch me trick myself in my own head, everyone is worried about ChatGPT ruining the art of writing meanwhile Grammarly was put on every university computer a decade ago, tap out and fight another day or injure your body to fail to protect your ego, I've never been so sure of absolutely nothing, there is an alternate universe where you fully believed in yourself, your dissatisfaction might be an evolutionary tool pushing you to do more with your life but what do I know, look at the habitats we're building now, are we trained circus animals or what, we're breaking through with this one boys, good and bad when it comes to art is entirely subjective but everyone knows crap when they smell it, pressurize your axons with a fierce firing of action potentials, I want my own silo full of grain, we used to worry about hidden microphones in the ceiling fan but now our phones take an infrared picture of our face every fifteen seconds and we shrug it off, what are you allowing to happen that is preventing what you want to happen, rekindle your cold heart, I don't like when people try to say what is because I feel like most is not what it seems, when were the moments where you were most uniquely you, you and me have a lot of catching up to do that we will never get to, it really is the most sensible thing to call yourself an idiot, we've all thought of packing the suitcase, we were just riding the high of being around each other, I hope I find forgiveness for any hurt that I've caused and if not I understand, I got done a few items on my to do list today, what'll we do if we run out of cheese, life is an incredible mystery and we will probably never know so make peace with what you can, unstoppable and continuous, how would you feel about your life if tomorrow kept being no different from today, a great deal of effort to spectacularly accomplish nothing, bouncing back from sheer calamity, every moment of the past has created this present but even my future will be ancient soon, what is on the other side of your coin, everything I own belongs to my cats, please bring me out of any uptight atmosphere and bring me where I can say some heinous shit without it really bothering anyone, we lost our pilot mid-flight, never by no means, I was in a band but we could never agree on a name, I've sounded genuinely stupid so many times, how big could the periodic table theoretically get, just don't be weird about it, if one man's trash is another man's treasure what does that say about my writing, every passing second with her seemed better than the last, just find a healthy way to enjoy yourself and let it run, you've been given the OK to pursue your ultimate fantasy, I'm thankful to have found an enjoyable way to spend my time, what evolutionary survival mechanism does madness fulfill, are you just a stencil being filled in or an original work of art, how exactly does one recover from utter devastation, that bitterness where even if you could you wouldn't, we can be both a watered seed and devoured prey, dogs can't see color but we can't smell for shit, pour an accelerant on your life and light the blaze, I'll be counting sheets of blank paper for the rest of my life, will we get past our differences or won't we, who keeps starting all these wars, make this year all about letting the year pass naturally, we deserve a fresh start don't we, what is a good life without some bad behavior, blow some bubbles this weekend, it is okay to like what you like, I wonder what twenty one twenty four will be like, will we live long enough to look back on any of this, we've always known reckless abandon but what about reasonable calculated abandon, amphibious airplanes, what'll you do when the lights go out, right now it feels like you're not going to make it but you will, spend ten years trying to crack a riddle that interests you, but what is up there and in there out there, is the opposite of paranoia just hope, I just want to be with you when the sun burns out, rearrange to a more comfortable position, we are just a very young species that thinks we know everything, they would have called me melancholic back in the day, you stirred up my neurons with a stick and they kept spinning, we wanted to be weird so we left the crowd, hey just calling to tell you I care about you please don't call me back, all I want is calm, they put me in a damn hypnogogic dream state, oh this guys crazy, travel further than the Earth has room for, I hope the legends are true, we are jumping off of buildings in more creative ways than ever, disappear up into the highest mountains you can find, you'll never ask the cost when your dream is earned, we got in some trouble for that fire, does anyone else's mind echo like this, light a bottle rocket off between your ass cheeks, we found the perfect spot, I can imagine the music, I'm not sure if you could say I'm well adjusted or not, one day it'll all be different so you really just have to learn to roll with it, if your wounds aren't healing you might need to see a specialist, I didn't intend to tear the page but it ripped anyway, not everyone sees their life's work come to fruition, if you overheard me talking and found me extremely annoying I am sorry, I'm trying to stop pontificating, don't let too many outside opinions color your own, that field of flowers has great grandparents that were flowers too, all I want to do is find a treasure map and quit my job in search of some doubloons, the only way to fully understand sacrifice is to feel pain and continue anyway, my reasons are valid and I don't need my reality challenged, I feel like no one is laying down thousand year prophecies like they used to, we are far behind and our future is coming, I'm not sure if I am comprehending the difference between interstellar and intergalactic distances, I would like to spend a week or two exploring the bottom of the ocean with lead shoes and gills, please spread my ashes where that type of thing is strictly prohibited, you'll start looking back on the present, I swear I'm going to find that missing piece of me, I want there to be aliens so bad, where do you think you'll end up once you truly try, cut loose from the last of your hang ups, which of your hurts have you already healed, I like people who can disagree with me without questioning my character, I hope I have one of those dreams that I am extremely good at skiing tonight, I just want my cats to stay off the kitchen counter I don't think it's too much to ask, we should start playing cooler music in elevators, check in with yourself periodically, an inadvertent accidental improvisational masterpiece, I heard someone refer to daydreaming as woolgathering and I don't want to forget that phrase so I'm writing it down here, glorious uninterrupted reverie, no matter how hard I try I keep dividing my attention, school really should not be so boring, be kind on your way up, there will never be a unanimous opinion ever again, welcome the phantoms when you've been lonely, how do we go about re-enchanting the disenchanted, don't worry about letting me down easy just knock me right over, no one was really at fault, our iPhones are going to make some strange antiques, who is the ringleader of you rabble rousers, instigate the maniacs, immaculate in each aspect, dealt with the woes but stuck with the bane, you could say it was a tolerable encounter, if they question my sanity their points may be valid but please hear my case, tell me which tenets you live by before you come in my house, are you merely entertaining your beliefs or are you prepared to die by each and every one of them, we got some decent rest, I have no collateral, will I end up doing anything good with my life, where is this book of tricks I keep hearing about, an audience of crickets performer beware, you'll be you every morning you wake up, you won't know how much you have to lose until you approach the edge of a very high cliff, and just like that another day is gone, can you point out one single case of a reputable person getting what they've always wanted by doing absolutely nothing, we are just one battle of an endless struggle, moving continents around like a game of checkers, take your time and explain your theory of who we are and why we are here, if you want a crisis of faith you will certainly get one, I want to learn what Odysseus learned, who has the right idea that wasn't heard, it is funny to think of someone with the worst intentions finding out about all the silver linings and good outcomes they accidentally caused, if you let me time travel I promise I will not change the past I just want to go see the pyramids in all their former glory, you will have to appreciate the good in spite of all the bad and that is an incredibly difficult thing to do, a productive moment of silence, I've got myself right where I want me, I've been using my microwave oven as a meditation timer, at what point should we re-evaluate our entire lives, I've never been that impressed by granite counter tops, I alternate back and forth between thinking there is nothing wrong with me and thinking there is something very wrong with me, I'm still young enough to be hopeful and I hope that sticks around for another decade or two, food grade anxiety and depression, just because you can recognize the horizon doesn't mean you're not lost, all you have to do is embrace the parts of you that you've been ignoring, why do my mistakes from elementary school keep bothering me so much, what we think will happen, can we know what we are, I grew up with wild blackberries in the back yard, if it has always been this bad then honestly I'm kind of scared, we agreed to the rules before we started playing, don't you dare blame the world for what you've done to yourself and stop blaming yourself for the pain inflicted on you by this cruel world, even if the apocalypse rained down on us I would still just write poetry and try to have a few laughs with whichever friends were still left, we know it can't be that good if it's easy but we still want it easy anyway, invest in a quality pair of headphones, friends who reassure you that you are doing alright, welp it looks like it wasn't even a good run, I'm addicted to getting the flu and having antibiotic fueled fever dreams, we forget even those obvious fairy tale lessons, to strive to be different and then find the people that align with that weirdness, do you ever ask too many questions, God bless the sore throat survivors, build an antigravity machine in your garage, it turns out there are positive consequences too, you don't get to pick and choose what you're meant to do, you would not believe what is hidden in the asteroid belt, I don't know if we have better access to information that we did sixty years ago or if we just have instantaneous access to what random people are saying about any subject which creates the illusion of more information but really it is just noise, writing poems while I'm cooking macaroni and cheese, something tells me God doesn't want us falling over and kissing their feet they just want us to be happy to see them, it certainly was a rude awakening but at least I'm not asleep anymore, are you making your ancestors proud or ashamed, looking out the window when it's dark outside, they tell me to think of nothing and instead I think for an hour about what the word nothing actually means, mental voyages, be careful with the deranged, thank you so much for listening to this crap, stop calling what you make garbage, tell your secrets to someone, we would all be shocked to find out what's really going on, how did the ancient people map out Antarctica's coast line, we've got random empty code in our DNA, coming home to a clean house, all I need is one good night's sleep, we will live through a total reorganization of the natural order, we often gloss over what matters most, you've found your place, the slow arduous and often fruitless process of trying to be a slightly better human being than the one you were yesterday, let all the cats out of all the bags, most of my imaginings have some major conflict baked into them, you thought a wave was coming but you got hit by a tsunami, a massive realization that you will never be able to turn away from, no one has ever said it quite like that, have you ever spent a significant amount of time around someone who just didn't understand your sense of humor, I might be an absolute idiot but that's totally okay, sitting illegally on the edge of the Eiffel tower, I want a doomsday bunker filled with my favorite books and movies, listen to what your dog is saying about you, the cathartic process of losing absolutely everything, you plant the seeds which grow the fruit of your own success or your own destruction, I'm only really in the present moment every now and then, we've got so much to live for but we've got to really be living, I had to sprint across thin ice to get here, bring a whoopie cushion into church next

Sunday, I would like to reiterate that it is never safe to assume, which hard decisions have you been avoiding recently, we've taken the quantum leap but somehow we're right back where we started, belonging is an important feeling, have your miraculous comeback montage, bring a torch from the light of your mind down into the furthest darkest reaches of your soul, there will come a time you finally feel exactly why you are alive, cross a desolate landscape with a ragtag trio, why is there a skyscraper out there in the middle of the desert, the strange place that is the interior of YOU, spend the next fifteen years cultivating a dynamic set of skills, go where you didn't think you could, it is time to accept that you are the living proof you needed, typos in my manuscript are just proof that none of this book was written by AI, raise your weapons above your head and scream until there is blood on the back of your teeth, would you rather be a gambler or a thief, is writing genetic, save the reef and clean the river, I love watching those documentaries about how quickly nature would reclaim everything if humans disappeared, we are not listening to the many lessons that our ancestors left for us, growth is slow during the process but appears instantaneous when looking back, live up to all the love you receive, protect your innocence, what is the human equivalent of chasing your own tail, you're safe now, burn sage, you've been looking so hard you're going to overlook it, where do we all go after this, I've come to quite enjoy my dissociations, living alongside the mighty hippopotamus for a decade, perfection is just an understanding of the flaws, she didn't need words when she could give me that look, a new take on an old classic, untether from your worries about the opinions of others and float off to where you are meant to be, I spent my entire day thinking about different combinations of beautiful words, the major importance of the smallest gesture, dedicate your time to what you love, life is hiding out on the dwarf planets, humans are adaptable so throw yourself into the situation you want to be in and then adapt to it, that's it we're moving to slab city, where can we go to leave society, in the spirit of those crazy bastards who first braved the high seas and inhabited all those tropical islands, has anyone ever gotten exactly what they expected, the further back we remember the more Gods and giants seemed to walk the Earth, we are nowhere near the pinnacle, the next step of evolution will not come until we have eliminated war and poverty, your grand dad was a little kid too, have you done everything in your power today, we are just dust and sticks held together with static, call her, every morning we wake up is another opportunity to do something with our lives, raw potential energy, I installed a trapdoor in my apartment and my downstairs neighbors are pissed, underneath your aggression is a scared child so you don't look cool or tough, your instincts are born from millions of years of evolution so you'd better take advantage and use them, you're one of a kind whether you think so or not, my bones do much of my talking, I like to both give and get a lot of slack in my conversations, it might not all totally work out but some of it will, she cleaned the snow off my car, there're a million different ways, a reminder of your mortality, what will you do with the rest of your time on the planet, how do I prevent my cats from jumping on the kitchen counter, I wonder if more coffee will make me feel better, I just so happened to find you right as I was finding myself, we didn't follow all the rules, I want to spend a year thinking under an elm tree, yesterday's choices, there will always be a mystery and someone to ask the questions, if it is all made up someone has got a damn good imagination, a good vibe frequency at an astounding rate, I've been practicing moving massive boulders with sound in my backyard but a federal agent came and told me to cease and desist immediately, combing through the wreckage of your soul's catastrophe, do you feel comfortable saying you've come a long way, I failed my own reality check, process your anger in the healthiest way that you can find, if humans could learn to be just a little bit more chill I could really see us getting along with the humpback whales, what is your audacious five year plan, loquacious yet precise, forever seeking that potent combination of ideas, are we really just a cloud of plankton hallucinating what life is like above the waves, strike up a secret romance, the music made by drops of water, bare the belly of your soul to the sky, laughing our way through the most painful points in our lives, follow the synchronicities to wherever they may lead, think and forget, novelty in the ordinary brought on by a fresh mindset and outlook, going back and forth will not get you there, consider all the places that you might end up in life and start moving towards the one that feels right, some of the group is bound to want to do what they are told not to do, you've been imprisoned in a pressurized dive suit deep in the Mariana trench, got a pocket full of rare enzymes, look what the human race is up to now, do mystery PowerPoint presentations with your friends, you are as cold as Antarctic ocean water, how many times has the laughing stock of the town been proven correct, if they tell us that aliens have invaded they are probably lying because the real aliens would never attack us, scientific scrutiny of the highly strange, have you ever seen that interstellar size comparison that shows how small our sun is, we are not as advanced as we believe ourselves to be, people used to lose their jobs if they reported their UFO sighting, solution of the enigma, look directly at the sun every morning, trust your instincts the way the cat always lands on its feet, close your eyes and envision your ultimate personal freedom and then make a list of steps that you can take to achieve that freedom, I found my intuition last year, you're going to have lines on your face from stress and laughter, we were unprepared for this amount of beauty, we have words to describe that which does not exist, what does this world want from me, surprise yourself with your own actions, withholding judgment is a virtue, if you were to fall from the sky where would you like to land, actually you didn't come up with that, each passing second creates the day, the wind on your butt cheeks, brand new notions, holding your future in your hands as it slowly melts, broken beyond repair is subjective according to what you are willing to fix, follow what pops into your mind each morning, go where you like the flavor of the fresh air, millions of brand new ways to say follow your heart, I guess it is as good of a time to rest as any, the eagle was bored so it explored the highest altitude it had ever soared, our souls badly want to float away but gravity keeps holding on, we talk just to fill up the air around us with ideas, either roll with the punches or get good at being punched in the face, remember that the pearl used to irritate the oyster, unfortunately I have to offer up the remaining years of my life as advertising space, chasing your goals is an ultramarathon not a go cart race, today we've decided to accept the love that we've been given, sacrifice who you want to be to receive who you are in return, hard work has always been worth it, view the world through the strangest camera lens you can find, all of this experience and our little chance to witness it, we can keep this one close to the chest, one day we were just here and one day we just won't be, unlimited mountaintops, ski the avalanche and surf the tsunami, come back with fresh eyes tomorrow, where're you goin' next, calling out your own mind for those tricks it plays, it only helps if you can relax while they pull your teeth, saying it all without quite saying it, what have you been refusing to let go, quitting your job is actually a great financial decision, you can't have my time but we can share a little bit of each other's, write until your legs are asleep and arthritis has your hand stuck in a claw, there shouldn't be anything in here you don't already know, petals of thought packed in intricate layers, we are only one small interaction of this complex organic algorithm, how silly of us to think that consciousness starts and ends with us, practice what you have learned through your many life lessons, cherish and exercise what freedoms you have, I'm going to wrap you loosely in a paper towel and microwave you for ninety seconds, we have a long way left to go but it's easier now that we've already gone a tremendous distance, the height of the pinnacle depends on the strength of the base, ensure the soil in which you are spreading your roots is rich with nutrients, google strangely profitable hobbies and start a shrimp farm in the Midwest, it is okay to want a new front lawn, we are standing on the precipice of a cliff that will change our lives forever, the study of the collapsing wave function and its application to the human life, as a human being you are born with an innate higher calling, sometimes we think humans are unnatural but then we come across the right angles of a bismuth crystal and suddenly our skyscrapers don't look that out of place, what used to be a monumental discovery is now a second thought, it really isn't any fun not knowing where the rent is coming from, leftover cold pasta, speed run the art museum, cheap clothes but momentum in your pockets, we went from daily hangovers to it's all over to I'll be right over, you'll know a new beginning when you see one, nothing will start happening for you until you face your fears, we're so deluded we need someone to come along and point out the obvious to us, I'm so thankful our lives crossed paths, I spent the entire day shooting hair elastics across the apartment for our cat, this spring will bloom our new life, write down everything you don't want to forget and everything you want to say, life will reliably rob us of our youth but will grant us a new perspective, creatures never seen before swimming in the depths of our soul, I'm thinking of training like sixty carrier pigeons, when you realize you've been dissociating to find your happy place, you might need to recalibrate what is worth fighting for and what needs letting go, sometimes you need someone to share your unhappiness for a second, I'm okay with being out of my mind, I'll never be able to thank you, they had me copying the bible when I had detention, only humans can try to describe what the spider might be feeling, your failures might be the most important part of your success, thankful for my access to clean spring water, keep company that wants you to be doing your best, we've been all Yin it's time for a little Yang, we survived not knowing any better, what we do not know is as important as what we do know especially because it includes all that we've yet to find out, a little prickly pear, we were supposed to be there a few hours ago, when you set out and search there is no telling what you'll find, how will I ever put my mind at ease after all of this, can you start a fire in the woods with nothing on you for survival, love has many different types and takes many different forms, I'm certain there is more, it's funny how hard it can be to quit what isn't even working for us, I have somewhat of an idea what I'll be doing with the rest of my life, will I be banished to the edge of infinity for eternity, save your own life, I can't seem to shut up about what I still don't know, we can only do so much from here, we'll go until all the pens run out of ink, for now we are separate but for the rest of time we won't be, are we sure there has ever been a path, what example have we set for ourselves, stare into the Hubble Deep Field picture and tell me what you see, reiterating my point about a few answers and new questions, for such a full sky it's awfully quiet, I would change my whole life around for you, all we could ever need plus a little left over, your place will come naturally, sometimes you'll have to fight the current but other times you can just lay on your back and float, squirm through, we were brought up on underdog stories and dangerously close calls, keep it all just above your heart, just because you don't understand doesn't mean nobody else does, fall like the mighty no matter your size, choose where you wisely put your effort, what is most important for us to hear is what we need to tell ourselves, take in as many vast vistas as you can, can you smell what I'm saying, today has always been the day, push yourself further than you ever thought you could go, a clear demonstration of value, your final moments will pass as easily as your first ones, I can see my own color being drained away, what exactly would it take to restore your faith in humanity, you're in charge of your biggest changes, I'm on my way, what would you have to give up for a totally fresh start, ten million tons of sadness lifted off your soul, I can easily be convinced, the ancient unsolved mystery of the human brain, if you could take one piece of this Earthly realm along with you when you die what would you bring, I'm learning to be grateful for the acorns and pinecones or the crickets and ladybugs, we can either quadruple down or start over and there's no way I'm starting over, you're going to have to acknowledge those hopes and dreams at some point, it'll all come down to a microsecond, one minute you're floating and the next you're falling, stumbling on the meaning of life completely by accident, we bought a new bookshelf, we found a burned up husk of an old shack in the middle of the woods, tell the kids that one day they will be excited about new furniture too, we will see an antigravity machine this century, you really don't have to be so hard on yourself anymore, I amazed myself out of the boredom that I was stuck in, all we have left is acceptance, wind me up and let me spin, we could've had limitless free energy for the entire planet but no one listened to Tesla, I'm sorry did I just ramble for an hour again, at some point you need to grow out of being an asshole, you're not a victim, we can survive hard times, being around a cynical prick is exhausting, grappling hook a passing shooting star, what is and isn't matters less and less, being on the run seems a lot better than being in hiding, we meet at the junction between faith and certainty, unhinged takes, don't ever count on eventually, where is the tallest tree in the forest, uncover all the hidden knowledge, grateful for the dishwasher and laundry machine today, butchering scientific theories with my limited vocabulary, I couldn't afford a copy editor, most of what can be called life is occurring below sea level, my brain could use a good wash, I hold free association practice every day at six thirty pm, we're definitely going to need a bigger frier for these fish, how still can we hold the wind, a well worn edge, we will laugh when we can and weep when we must, how many times will we see the sun set and rise, acceptance of the course of events, many types of entities converge in our unique dimension, look at the incredible variety of what occurs naturally, full sails, buts and ors change the whole direction of the thought, should I just burn this manuscript in a trashcan, why do we see it all one at a time when really it is happening all at once, humans were much smarter ninety thousand years ago, no one is going to believe us when we talk about our lives here on Earth, you're bound to be blown away, what color were all those ancient monuments in their heyday, it is okay to say never, opposing environments, I keep trying to think of what I probably cannot know, I'll run until my mind is tired, real life fairy tales are happening right now, our one remaining shot at redemption, what will you do when the coastline changes, what is happening in the center of the observable universe, what is the Richat structure, with so much waiting to be discovered what will you go look for, even granite gives way eventually, I'm certain giants used to roam the Earth, we should build eight billion hot showers for everyone to use freely, just do all you're capable of doing, I hope to see you soon, a sound that has never been heard, what I wouldn't give to trade places with a bald eagle for forty five minutes, everything is forgotten but you never know what will be randomly remembered, our explanations are insufficient, I will say more when I can, I wrote this hoping to become a better writer but what if it only made me better at speaking absolute nonsense, assumptions lead to miscalculations and failures, happiness from within is the most useful happiness, I am proud of the work that I have done so far, the difference between clever and genius is the number of live the intelligence effects, I will hear out your argument if you agree to hear out my own, we broke through all of our blockages and now we only run free and clear, elbow grease given away for free, I found all the words I needed to say and now I'm trying to get all of them said, how is it all just randomly this perfect, wonder is endless, positivity will burn away the doubt, what is hidden deep within the Grand Canyon, what is our galaxy thinking about, reality is alive, find a healthy obsession, the happiest people get sad too, remember that time you broke that bone, churning neurons, a sign of life against a stark empty landscape, show me the back room of the museum, learn how to give no as an answer and accept no as a response, seek to better understand the changes in your life, you're just one in a trillion times a trillion, just wait until I start writing stuff that makes sense

♫

There is no proper ending to this work, you can just start over if you want.

Thank you for reading.

Use these pages to exercise your own conscious stream.

RAW MATERIAL

Thank You for Existing

You matter, whether you think so or not. The cells in your body are working together right now to actively keep you alive, to keep *you* being *you*, a living breathing human being.

We have the ability to think, to exercise our consciousness, to dream, to plan, to change our perspective, or to change our entire lives.

If you find yourself here on this planet, reading this book, in whatever dusty corner of the world you might momentarily occupy, there might be a profound reason for it. You don't know what will happen tomorrow, or a week from now, or a year from now, but there might be a purpose, you might even save someone's life one day. You might be walking down the street and see a car driving the wrong way, and push someone you've never met to safety. You have no idea.

Life could really suck right now, but you might have a purpose in a decade that is impossible to perceive through all of the current bullshit.

Take care of yourself, push yourself, ask more of yourself, go easy on yourself, bet on yourself, forgive yourself, redeem yourself, discover yourself, calm yourself, teach yourself.

Expand your consciousness, write the book, write the screenplay, throw the paint at the wall, call your friend, make the video, make the song, learn a new instrument, take the class, get the degree, build a black belt.

Let this be your time.

FIND THESE LINES

These are my favorite lines in the book, in no particular order. Try to find them!

1. Today I am going to sit with all the emotions that I've been running from
2. An orchestral cell phone ring tone
3. You're a force of nature through your frontal lobe alone
4. Windows open please
5. We are sitting on a muddy little rock spinning around a ball of fire
6. The true breakthrough in lucid dreaming comes when you're awake
7. Imagine if it works
8. Don't idolize just respect
9. Send me to the lunar prison colony
10. Would you rather understand more or be understood better
11. Part of me is terrified so I'm working on the other part of me
12. You are just as valid of a person as anyone else who has lived and breathed

13. I hope you escape the rat race and find unlimited cheese
14. If we are an experiment then let our lives yield unprecedented results
15. We used to read the back of the cereal box we were so bored
16. It really is unfathomable why we exist at all
17. Poach yourself like an egg in a steam room and take a dangerously long nap
18. Charter a space shuttle
19. Did you ever end up finding your wheel house
20. Fever dream journal
21. A terrible thing about the internet is that you cannot properly size up who is attacking you
22. All my best homies have tinnitus
23. Praise all the broken brains that keep thinking anyway
24. We are so worried about computers gaining sentience when we seem to be valuing our own sentience less than ever
25. We are massively under-utilizing the human potential
26. Some knowledge is unavoidable
27. Maybe I don't actually exist
28. What would you do with your mental freedom if you had it

29. We've been all Yin for a while it's time for a little Yang
30. I had to sprint across thin ice to get here
31. Positivity will burn away the doubt
32. The fact that you can feel more energized from exercise is hard to understand from an out of shape perspective
33. Rescue you from you
34. If your friends never encourage you then they're not your friends
35. Never shy away
36. I have a goal not a dream or fantasy
37. With a single step missing from a thousand-mile journey you will not arrive
38. Our cities smell like humans
39. Awe and wonder are proven to be beneficial to your mental health
40. I'm so glad I grew up with a trampoline
41. It's totally okay to look like a fool
42. Don't forget to do goon shit with your friends

ACKNOWLEDGEMENTS

Thank you to all my friends and family for encouraging me to write.

Thank you specifically, Jamie, Magnet, and Wednesday, for the direct moral support.

Thank you to all the people who have read my writing thus far. Each word of feedback, praise, and criticism, has meant people are reading my words, which makes me feel like my absolutely insane compulsion to write is worth all the time and effort.

Every conversation that I find myself in, that I probably wouldn't be having otherwise, due to my writing also makes it worth doing.

I will continue for all of you.

About the Author

Tucker K Sullivan is a writer, storyteller, and poet. He struggled with hallucinations and delusions in his teenage years, and into his early twenties. Lucky for him, he leveled off and started writing. He also went back to school to study psychology and learn how best to help others like him. He now tries to do that through his words.

His first book is a collection of poetry he self-published called ***Relate! One Human to Another***.

Raw Material is his second book.

He also has a blog, where he writes about human existence. He has social media, where he posts videos of skiing, rollerblading, poetry, cats, fireworks, motorcycles, and other bullshit with his friends.

He goes by @tuckerksullivan on all platforms, and has a website:

www.tuckersullivan.com.

www.ingramcontent.com/pod-product-compliance
Lightning Source LLC
Chambersburg PA
CBHW060552080526
44585CB00013B/537
* 9 7 8 1 7 3 5 9 5 8 5 3 8 *